THE TYPE OF *Marriage* THAT *Endures*

THE TYPE OF *Marriage* THAT  *Endures*

CRAIG GLEERUP

Tate Publishing & Enterprises

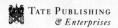
TATE PUBLISHING
& *Enterprises*

Tate Publishing is committed to excellence in the publishing industry. Our staff of highly trained professionals, including editors, graphic designers, and marketing personnel, work together to produce the very finest books available. The company reflects the philosophy established by the founders, based on Psalms 68:11,

"THE LORD GAVE THE WORD AND GREAT WAS THE COMPANY OF THOSE WHO PUBLISHED IT."

If you would like further information, please contact us:
1.888.361.9473 | www.tatepublishing.com
TATE PUBLISHING & *Enterprises*, LLC | 127 E. Trade Center Terrace
Mustang, Oklahoma 73064 USA

The Type of Marriage that Endures

MBTI® and MYERS-BRIGGS TYPE INDICATOR® are registered trademarks and MYERS-BRIGGS™ is a trademark of Consulting Psychologists Press, Inc., the publisher of the MBTI instrument.

All scripture quotations are taken from the *New American Standard Bible*®, Copyright © 1960, 1962, 1963, 1968, 1971, 1972, 1973, 1975, 1977, 1995 by The Lockman Foundation. Used by permission. All rights reserved.

This book is designed to provide accurate and authoritative information with regard to the subject matter covered. This information is given with the understanding that neither the author nor Tate Publishing, LLC is engaged in rendering legal, professional advice. Since the details of your situation are fact dependent, you should additionally seek the services of a competent professional.

Published in the United States of America

ISBN: 1-5988678-3-0

07.01.03

DEDICATION

To my Lord Jesus Christ, who loved me when I was unlovable, forgave me when I was unforgivable, and found me when I was lost.

To my beautiful wife, Regina, and my lovely daughters Katie and Samantha, who endure my spontaneous, live-for-the-moment personality.

ACKNOWLEDGEMENT

I would like to express deep gratitude for the generous help of my friend and personal editor, Jill McKay. Jill is one of the sweetest people I know, who unselfishly extends herself for others without the expectation of affirmation or recognition. Though she would never mention it, I must frustrate her with mistakes in the manuscript that should be corrected prior to her receiving her copy. May the Lord bless all of her endeavors.

I would like to thank Tate Publishing for giving me the opportunity to strengthen marriages through the written word. Every person I have dealt with at Tate has shown nothing more than the joy of the Lord in their heart.

My appreciation also goes out to those pastors who initially gave me the opportunity to begin the ministry of MBTI and marriage in their churches: Pastor Roger Putman of Franklin, Kentucky; Pastors Larry and Janet Herbert of Springfield, Tennessee; and Pastor Harvey Kirby of Lafayette, Tennessee.

A special thanks goes to my prayer partner and fellow author, John Revell. His guidance, inspiration, and friendship are invaluable.

TABLE OF CONTENTS

Chapter 1

WHY TYPE A MARRIAGE?

"Jesse comes home from work and ignores me and the children."

"Vickie always wants to go out with friends, I'd rather stay home and spend time with her alone."

"Harry wants to plan the whole weekend by Wednesday. I'd rather see what I am in the mood to do when the weekend is here."

"Rachel won't ever talk to me about issues; she just walks off by herself."

"Jack won't make a decision."

"Juanita always waits until the last minute."

"Danny gets his feelings hurt too easily and wants to talk about it."

"Stacy changes her mind constantly."

Any of these situations sound familiar to you? Chances are you or someone you know has made similar statements. In some cases, these situations can actually become irritants in a marriage that can fester into larger problems. So large, in fact, that over time they can lead to divorce. Though we may become irritated with some of the behaviors of our spouse, the behaviors may be driven from a gift from God, called personality type.

Personality type is a gift that is given to us from God at conception that stays with us throughout our lifetime. It is a natural preference within us that causes us to think and act in a certain way. For example, some people have an innate desire to organize and plan, while others have a preference to do things on the spur of the moment. Some have tendencies to be more social and want to talk about issues immediately, while others prefer to be less social and think about issues thoroughly before talking about them. There are types of people who prefer to deal with concepts and theories, while others would rather get into the details of a matter. Then there are those who prefer to consider decisions logically while others seem to make decisions based more on people or their emotions. These preferences make up our distinct personalities.

All of these differences in personality are part of God's wonderful plan: His body of believers with differing parts, each functioning in its own unique way together for His purpose.

> *For the body is not one member, but many. If the foot says, "Because I am not a hand, I am not a part of the body," it is not for this reason any the less a part of the body. And if the ear says, "Because I am not an eye, I am not a part of the body," it is not for this reason any less a part of the body. If the whole body were an eye, where would the hearing be? If the whole were hearing, where would the sense of smell be? But now God has placed the members, each one of them, in the body, just as He desired. If they were all one member, where would the body be?* (1 Cor. 12:14–19)

It's obvious that we as humans cannot change our own body parts to function in a way other than they were designed. For example, we can't train our livers, gall bladders, and kidneys to act as a heart. We can't reconstruct our hands, arms, and fingers to function as a nose. Each organ has a particular function and place—and all work together for the good of our body. Like the organs, God has a desire for us as His people to work together as one, each with the unique gifts He has given us; therefore we cannot and should not attempt to change one another's innate personality.

Although we cannot change one's personality type, people can and do learn behaviors that may be opposite of our preferences. For example, there are men who are spontaneous that will do quite well at planning to attend a sporting event where the advance purchase of tickets is necessary. There are women who prefer to be spontaneous who will spend countless hours planning a wedding.

Although we can learn behaviors or actions that are not our personality preferences, we generally will revert to our personality preferences throughout much of our lives. Working to change the personality of our spouse is counter to God's gifting. Realistically, it can be dangerous to attempt changing someone's personality. Forcing someone to hide their preferences and consistently act in a manner other than their preferences can lead to additional stress in a marriage.

Understanding why people act as they do and learning how to work together can be complicated, yet there are basic tools that we can use to understand our spouse's personality type. This is the first step to living in unity with your spouse and with God.

The most widely used and respected tools for determining personality type is called the Myers-Briggs Type Indicator. This tool helps the individual to identify particular personality types so we may develop strategies to work together rather than work against one another.

MYERS-BRIGGS TYPE INDICATOR

The Myers-Briggs Type Indicator, or MBTI, was designed by a mother-daughter team of Katherine Briggs and Isabel Briggs-Myers. Together they designed an instrument that was intended to make the work of Swiss psychiatrist Carl Jung both understandable and useful to the average person or groups.[1] Since their intent was to simplify the tool and make it useful, I will bypass the technical explanation of how the MBTI works and much of the history behind it. It will be more beneficial to spend our time learning the basics of the tool and how we as adults can benefit from it.

The MBTI is basically a set of questions that helps us identify some of the distinct personality preferences in which a person has been gifted by God. It looks a lot like a test, but there are no right or wrong answers. The answers given by an individual are used to identify "possible" preferences in the personality. These are possible preferences because an individual can over-ride the results by declaring themselves to have preferences other than what is shown on the MBTI results.

All of this may sound confusing, but as we look at the individual preferences, you will begin to have the sense for where you and your spouse may lie in the preference dichotomies.

WHY TYPE A MARRIAGE?

About ten years ago, I surprised my wife with a romantic weekend for the two of us. I thought she would be ecstatic. Instead, I was met with stunned silence and a little frustration for the first six hours of the trip.

Before you begin to blame my wife for the trip not starting out well, let me take the blame. The problem stemmed from my lack of knowledge of her personality preferences, even though we had been married for eight years. In fact, I didn't understand what had happened that weekend until a few years later when I became familiar with Myers-Briggs. The less-than-desirable results were due to my ignorance, and I have been able to avoid this problem ever since. Let me continue with my story to illustrate the need for typing a marriage.

One spring morning my wife woke up terrified because she realized the baby monitor was off. As any good mother would, she panicked with thoughts of our one-year-old daughter crying out throughout the night. As she bolted from the bedroom, she noticed my daughter and me playing together on the living room floor.

"What are you doing home?" she asked with grave concern.

"I took the day off," I replied.

"Did you get fired?"

It didn't take me long to understand that she was not comprehending what was happening. I thought it was the "cleaning the cobwebs out after you awaken" syndrome. Calmly, I said, "No, I *took* the day off."

"How come?" she asked completely lost as to why I would use one of those precious days of vacation.

Proudly I stated, "I planned a romantic get-away weekend for us."

"Where to?" she asked.

"It's a surprise."

"Well, I had plans today," she said, totally disregarding my romantic notion.

"I know. You mentioned to me several times what you were going to do today, so I took care of your tasks already."

"Well . . . who's going to take care of the baby?"

"Your mother already agreed to take her for the weekend," I said.

"Well . . . how do I pack since I don't know where I'm going?" she asked.

I said, "Pack like you normally do . . . pack everything."

Obviously, that statement didn't go over quite as humorously as I intended. She began to pack with an internal battle brewing: she wanted to be upset with me for disrupting her plans for the day, but at the same time, she was pleased with me for loving her enough to plan a surprise romantic weekend.

As I drove to a historic bed and breakfast, located off the town square in a small Kentucky town, my wife rode in silence. No matter how hard I tried, I could not engage her in any meaningful conversation. When we arrived, we found our room to be the grandest in the building. The room was usually reserved for honeymooners, complete with all the amenities reserved for those in love. Regina was only slightly impressed.

After settling in, we took a drive around the quaint little town in search of the best restaurant. Nothing seemed to impress her, so we went back to the room and decided to walk around the historic square area of downtown and find a restaurant there. She still couldn't find anything to her liking and asked me to pick one.

"This one looks good," I said.

"I bet it doesn't have much on the menu," she said disappointed.

We settled down to a menu that was more like a book with its six pages of deliciously described food. Regina ordered and said little else. As the waiter brought wave upon wave of food to our table, I could see her shoulders slump as the tension began to fade. She was planning the rest of the weekend in her mind.

"The food here is really good and I'm surprised at how much they had on the menu," she said with a completely different tone than she had used all day. "I was thinking, after dinner we could take the horse-drawn carriage ride at the square. It could take us around town to see the historic sites. Then we could relax for the evening. Tomorrow, we could walk to a few of the sites and look at them more closely."

She had finally bought into the notion that this was a weekend for enjoyment and romance. She ended up enjoying the trip so much I didn't think I would get her to leave when it was time to check out. What I didn't know then was that I upset her need for planning by not giving her time to internally process or think about the trip. Once she internally thought about plans for the rest of the weekend, *that* is when she relaxed and had a good time.

In chapters three and four we will discover exactly what the issues were that caused the trip to start off on such a sour note and what issues caused it to recover. Knowing these strategies has helped me to understand my wife better and avoid making poor decisions in the future. In other words, it changed how I approach my wife.

CHANGING YOUR OWN STRATEGY

What Myers-Briggs taught me was that the personality preferences my wife received at birth were the same ones she would maintain throughout her life. Changing her is not an option, as many of you have figured out about your own spouse. Sure, there can be some growth and some behavior changes through life, but the innate preferences will stay basically the same. Therefore, I have to take the approach of altering my strategies for dealing with my spouse rather than attempting to change her.

Often when teaching business classes on Myers-Briggs basics, I find people who see their spouse in a type that is different from their own. I can tell by their questions that they are trying to figure out how they can "fix" their spouse toward their own type, as if one personality type is better than another. When I see that, I quickly correct their assumptions.

Since type doesn't change, the premise is on the person to alter their own strategies on dealing with the other half of their marriage. I often give counsel to married couples to find a way to alter their own individual behavior to accommodate their spouse as long as they don't always try to stay in a behavior that is opposite of their own preference.

The problem with one person always flexing their natural behavior to accommodate a spouse is that it causes a rise in fatigue and stress on the accommodating spouse. According to Katharine D. Myers and Linda K. Kirby, tension (or stress) increases as one acts outside of his natural preference. They also add that continued feedback that one's preferences are wrong can lead to devastation of one's confidence.[2]

I continue to enjoy having romantic weekends away with my wife. In fact, she enjoys them more now that I have changed my strategy in initiating them. The weekends no longer start off as a surprise; now she is part of the planning of the trip. Sure, I can surprise her in other ways—just as long as I do not alter her plans significantly.

TYPE UNDERSTANDING LEADS TO WISDOM

What makes knowledge and understanding effective is when they are applied with wisdom. Wisdom, in the biblical sense, is more of a skill than a cognitive function as is commonly believed. God spoke to Moses, as it is written in the thirty-first chapter of Exodus, and told him of the men He provided that were full of "wisdom" to build the tabernacle. The Hebrew word translated into wisdom here is *chokmah*, which refers to skill. When Solomon asked for wisdom, it was consummated when he *applied* it through a leadership decision in response to a confrontation between two women. The key here is that wisdom is the application of the knowledge and understanding. Understanding of personality type can lead one to wisdom or skill in applying the principles to accomplish harmony in relationships.

Developing a new strategy that applies personality type principles can strengthen a marriage full of wisdom. Again, this is not manipulation of your spouse; it is working in a spirit of harmony and love. My wife appreciates my knowing her preferences in a deeper way because this illustrates my love and devotion to her.

I overheard my wife on more than one occasion tell friends that they should allow me to teach them the Myers-Briggs basics. She explains, "He now knows how to handle me." Now some ladies may feel offended by that statement, thinking that I manipulate her. That isn't my intention, nor is that how she receives it. Her thoughts are more along the lines of my understanding her needs and accommodating them.

My wife's needs are different than mine, and by understanding her needs, I can alter my strategy to help her work within her preferences more of the time. For example, she has a need to think things through internally *before* making a decision. When at all possible, I give her time to formulate an answer before asking for her opinion. She also prefers to have plans. I offer her time to plan for something as major as a car purchase or vacation or as minor as what to eat for supper.

I had lunch one day with a pastor and his wife. I did not realize that their marriage was not well. A couple of weeks after having lunch and talking to them about personality type, he called me to tell me how much of an impact that lunch had on his marriage.

"You need to teach Myers-Briggs at my church," he said. "You have made a real difference in my life."

"That's great," I said.

"No, you really don't understand," he said. "You saved my marriage in that hour and a half for lunch. We had stayed together because I am a pastor and that's what we were supposed to do. But, the past couple of weeks have been terrific, and I want the rest of my church to experience the same."

What made a difference in their marriage was the fact that each person gained a deeper understanding of the other and applied wisdom in their handling of the other. I have seen it happen to other couples since then, and it excites me to the point of becoming the focus of my ministry. My focus is to be used by God for the fulfillment of Jesus' prayer recorded in John chapter seventeen.

The glory which You have given Me I have given to them, that they may be one, just as We are one; I in them and You in Me, that they may be perfected in unity . . . (John 17:22–23a)

Without the "one-mind" mentality, even Christian marriages can fail. According to Christian research group, The Barna Group, born-again Christians are as likely to divorce as the general population. "Among married born again Christians, 35% have experienced a divorce. That figure is identical to the outcome among married adults who are not born again: 35%."[3] This is in spite of the churches attempts to deter members from divorcing.

These divorce rates indicate that we need to do more to lower the divorce rate with believers. It is written in Hosea 4:6 that God's people perish for a lack of knowledge. It is my attempt to help improve marriages through a greater knowledge of self and of spouses. So, enough with the need for understanding personality type, it is time to venture into the tool of understanding—the Myers-Briggs Type Indicator.

Chapter 2

THE MYERS-BRIGGS TYPE INDICATOR

Carl Jung was an Austrian-born psychiatrist. In the early 1900s he identified a few consistencies in human behavior that he determined were preferences. These preferences were dichotomous in nature. In other words, each preference had polar opposites. For example, a person had a natural preference to plan or to be spontaneous. Jung published his findings that are referred to as Jungian theory which formed the basics for the Myers-Briggs Type Indicator.

A few in the Christian circles have concerns about Jung's theories since he is not readily identified as a Christian. Because of this, some leaders in the church have shunned the idea of using the MBTI, because Katherine Briggs and Isabel Briggs-Myers drew information from a non-Christian. These people will deny the substantial scientific validation of the tool because of who discovered it. Yet, many of these same people will watch CNN, a news network that was created by Ted Turner, an avowed atheist. They will use their Microsoft products that were the brainchild of Bill Gates who does not claim to be born-again. And, many of you who turned on the light to read this book have done so as a result of the work of avowed atheist, Thomas Edison.

We have to consider that truth is truth whether it is discovered by a Christian or identified by a non-Christian. In the book, *Knowing Me,*

Knowing God, Malcolm Goldsmith put it this way, "As I already pointed out, it [Myers-Briggs Type Indicator] is not a specifically Christian instrument any more than a motor car, word processor, or electric light, but like those examples many Christians use it and have been helped by it."[4] So as Jung identified differences in personality, we need to gain understanding of how God desires for us to use our differences.

THE TRUTH ABOUT OUR DIFFERENCES

Paul wrote to the believers at Corinth illustrating how God's people operate like one human body. In chapter 12 in his second letter to the Corinthians, Paul made four major points about the body. The four points are:

+ All the parts of the body are under the direction of one God.

+ Each part is important yet depends on the other parts.

+ The parts must operate uniquely.

+ There should not be any divisions in the body.

Let's look at each of these four points individually.

Since our personality is a gift given by God, it should be directed by God. Paul writes:

> Now there are a variety of gifts, but the same Spirit. And there are a variety of ministries, and the same Lord. There are varieties of effects, but the same God who works all things in all persons. (1 Corinthians 12:4–6)

In the King James Version of this passage the word for "effects" is translated as "operations." The original Greek word is "energema" or the energy of work. In other words, the verse is saying that there are a variety of ways in which energy of work is directed. Personality preferences being gifts from God, are directed by God. We do not pick and chose what our personality becomes. We are born with the type preferences we have and maintain them through life. Although many feel their personality preferences change through their life, they in fact learn how to work better in their non-preferred areas as they mature. Still, the energy of work directed by each part of Christ's body is directed by God, meaning that each of us has a unique way in which God wants us to direct our energies.

Paul's second point was clear that each part of the body is important. Look at any successful sports team and you will find a variety of players with unique talents, size, speed, and mentality. The role that each team member plays within a team is important.

In basketball, for example, you have a center that is usually taller than the rest of the team and plays close to the basket. Typically, the center is not a good ball handler and is encouraged not to dribble the ball where it is often stolen by the opposing team. Conversely, the point guard is the ball-handler who is usually quicker and shorter than the center. This position also tends to direct the team plays and is located away from the basket. The roles of these players can shift in the game for a short period of time to surprise the other team, but for most of the game, the players know their roles and play those roles well.

God created each person with personality preferences that are differing. The purpose is so we will play a variety of roles in the family of God. Not all people are leaders, not all are helpers, not all have a knack for counseling, and so on. Each role and the differences in them is important. Paul noted this when he was referring to spiritual gifts that God gives. The importance resides in the use for the common good of mankind and the distribution of them as God wills.

> *But to each one is given the manifestation of the Spirit for the common good. But one and the same Spirit works all these things, distributing to each one individually just as He wills.* (1 Corinthians 12:7, 11)

The third point Paul makes in this chapter is the need for the uniqueness of one another. He writes:

> For even the body is one and yet many members, and all the members of the body, though they are many, are one body, so also is Christ. But now God has placed the members each one of them, in the body, just as He desired. If they were all one member, where would the body be? (1 Corinthians 12:12, 18–19)

For where would the body (or all those who belong to Christ) be if all were exactly alike? All of the matters of the church or family or business would not be handled if we did not depend on others to accomplish things through their unique talents and preferences. The variety of tasks such as accounting, organizing, housekeeping, and childcare each require a unique set of skills. None of us have the *all* the skills necessary to successfully accomplish *all* the work.

The first three points Paul made are moot unless the last issue is addressed. There should be no divisions in the body. We must be directed by God, understanding the uniqueness of each other's personality preferences and allowing each preference to be used for His glory without creating division.

> So that there may be no division in the body, but that the members may have the same care for one another. And if one member suffers, all the members suffer with it; if one member is honored, all the members rejoice with it. (1 Corinthians 12:6–7)

Myers-Briggs identifies personality preferences for the purpose of understanding rather than division. Some may challenge as to the purpose of classifying individuals to better understand them. It can look like profiling or categorizing people to discriminate. However, we gladly classify people to in certain situations. One of these classifications our society relies on regularly is female gender. With this "profiling" we can study issues distinct with the female gender to produce books focused on women's health or women's self-help issues. Without classifying the gender and studying traits that are typical to that special group of people, those books would not exist. That would limit the help available to women. Myers-Briggs identifies groups with similar preferences so that we may understand others better and learn how to better communicate, teach, and love in a way that each person appreciates.

As with any tool, you can use it or misuse it. A hammer can be used as a tool to build a house, or it can be used as a weapon to kill. The Bible can be used to help one another understand God and His love for us, or it can be used to constantly brow-beat others. Myers-Briggs can be used to understand others, or it can be used to limit someone or give excuse for poor behavior. I recommend we use the tool to equip the church for better service to all of mankind.

> *For the equipping of the saints for the work of service, to the building up of the body of Christ.* (Ephesians 4:12)

THE IDENTIFIERS THAT CATEGORIZE

To illustrate the dichotomies of type and how they work, try this exercise. With a pen or pencil write your first and last name on a piece of paper. For the second step, place the pen or pencil in your other hand and write your name again.

Generally what you will find is that even though you can write your name with both hands, the second time took more thought to accomplish and it didn't feel as comfortable to write. In addition, the second time probably doesn't look as good as the first. For some of you doctors, you didn't think your writing could be worse, but it can. This exercise is a good illustration to the "either or" dichotomies that are the identifiers of personality preference.

Dichotomies can be illustrated as a line. On one end of the line you can write the word left-handed and the other end you can write the word right-handed. The right of the midpoint of the line represents those who prefer to use their right hand. Left of the midpoint represents those who prefer to use their left hand.

Some people are very clear about being right-handed while other right-handers are more adept to using the left hand. They are still right-handed, but they have learned to use the left hand more and not depend entirely on the right hand. This would determine where on the dichotomy the clarity of right-handedness would fall. The clear right-hander would fall more toward the far right of the line while the one who is more adept with the left hand would fall more toward the middle. One would be able to improve the performance of the left-hand, but their natural tendency would always be to use their right hand. Therefore, they would still be on the right side of the dichotomy.

FOUR DICHOTOMIES OF MBTI

The dichotomies of Myers-Briggs work much the same as our right-hand, left-hand dichotomy. Myers-Briggs has four unique dichotomies of personality preferences. Each one focuses on a particular aspect of preference. However, the four are not completely independent of one another. They work together to create a variety of sixteen different personality types.

The first dichotomy is where we get our direction of energy. On one side of the dichotomy are the people who prefer to recharge their batteries internally by spending time alone. On the other side are those people who get recharged by spending time discussing matters with others. This is the difference between introverts and extraverts. Contrary to popular belief, introversion does not mean one who is shy and doesn't talk much. Also, extraversion doesn't mean that a person is talkative. In the next chapter, we will discuss in more detail the real meaning behind introversion and extraversion.

Myers-Briggs Dichotomies

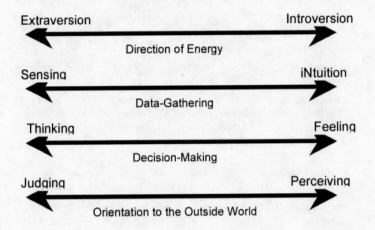

The next dichotomy or category of preference is Data-Gathering. In data-gathering, the preference is based on how we gather information through our five senses. Even though we all use the same five senses to gather information, the difference is in the perspective we use to filter the information we gather. Several individuals can look at the same object and see something different. The data-gathering dichotomy explains some of the differences in our perspective.

The third dichotomy is the decision-making function. Some people use mostly logic in making their decisions, while others are more influenced by how the decision will affect others. This preference identifies how our brain prefers to make decisions based on the data we gathered in the previous function.

How we prefer to orient ourselves to the outside world is the last dichotomy. In this preference, we separate ourselves by those who prefer to plan the day and stick to the plan versus those who like to be more spontaneous. The spontaneous person may make a plan, but prefer to have options in the plan, so if his mood changes, his plan can change.

The combination of the four dichotomies is dynamic in their relationship to one another. For example, a spontaneous person who prefers extraversion will look a little different than a spontaneous person who prefers introversion. Also, an introvert will act on planning differently than an extravert will. What happens is a dynamic interaction of the four dichotomies that identify sixteen unique personality types that is known as Myers-Briggs.

ISTJ	ISFJ	INFJ	INTJ
Introverted Sensing Thinking Judger	Introverted Sensing Feeling Judger	Introverted iNtuitive Feeling Judger	Introverted iNtuitive Thinking Judger
ISTP	**ISFP**	**INFP**	**INTP**
Introverted Sensing Thinking Perceiver	Introverted Sensing Feeling Perceiver	Introverted iNtuitive Feeling Perceiver	Introverted iNtuitive Thinking Perceiver
ESTP	**ESFP**	**ENFP**	**ENTP**
Extraverted Sensing Thinking Perceiver	Extraverted Sensing Feeling Perceiver	Extraverted iNtuitive Feeling Perceiver	Extraverted iNtuitive Thinking Perceiver
ESTJ	**ESFJ**	**ENFJ**	**ENTJ**
Extraverted Sensing Thinking Judger	Extraverted Sensing Feeling Judger	Extraverted iNtuitive Feeling Judger	Extraverted iNtuitive Thinking Judger

Keep in mind that preferences do not necessarily equal specific behavior. Myers-Briggs does not predict behavior, it identifies unique preferences. There are other factors that can affect our specific behavior. For example, as a child, I was taught to function with more of an introverted style than my extraverted preference was yearning for. I learned the behavior, but it did not change my personality. What it did was increase my stress by not being able to extravert. In time, I found avenues outside of the home to express my need to extravert. Many times the need to extravert caused me to gather with others that were a poor influence on me.

REDUCING STRESS AND FATIGUE

Understanding the type of a person and providing them with an outlet to express their preferences will lessen their stress and fatigue—especially for your spouse. Stress and fatigue can be caused by functioning continually outside of one's preferences. In listening to many people who express problems in their marriages, they indicate a real frustration with their spouse's preference and feel somewhat oppressed by not being able to express their own preferences. As you will see in the following chapters, challenges can occur when an extravert is not given a chance to ever talk things out or when an introvert is always forced to talk things out before being given a chance to think things over. Other challenges occur when one spouse goes into great detail in relating on the events of the day, when the other spouse prefers to hear the general events without the specific detail.

Marriages flourish when both partners in a marriage understand each other's needs and compromise to allow the free expression of both parties. Let's get started by understanding the attitude of the direction of energy.

Chapter 3

THE DIRECTION OF ENERGY

A couple I know would have small disagreements that would very quickly escalate into full-blown arguments early in their marriage. In most cases, it wasn't so much the issue that would cause it to escalate it was how they handled the discussion that was the problem.

The typical fight would result in the husband's desire to talk things out and address issues right away. In his mind there was no need to let things linger and go unresolved. So when an issue arose, he would jump right in and begin a discussion with his wife. His frustration would increase, since he could see that the discussion would immediately become tense and not very cooperative.

Voices would begin to rise and she would become quite defensive. The discussion would seem to go directly to who was right and who was wrong. He claims his intent was not to discover right and wrong. In fact, most situations between a husband and wife are not about right and wrong, they are usually about one's preference verses the other's preference. So, his desire was to discuss the issue so they could gain an understanding of each other's view and respect it with understanding. However, it seemed that she would suddenly lose all sense of rationality. To "help" her understand his point, he would resort to asking simple questions to force her logic. It would go something like this:

"Think about it, when were we married?" He asks in an attempt to gain some agreement between them.

"I don't know," she replies.

With his anger quickly rising for not answering such a simple question, he asks "You don't know when we were married?"

"I just can't think about it off the top of my head right now," she says.

At this point, he wonders what there is to think about, but he holds off on a response like that and attempts to get the discussion back on track. His next question makes it so simple that she can't miss it.

"Well, we were married on September eighth, right?"

"I just don't know anymore," she says with marked frustration.

At this point, he loses it and there is no more rational discussion on this argument or anything else for the next few days.

The problem is not actually the wife in this situation. Even though the husband wants to work toward a solution, he is not taking into consideration the best way for her to discuss matters of importance (and in some cases, unimportance). His intention is good. The problem is due to his lack of knowledge of personality preferences.

The source of the problem in this case is the differences in the direction of energy between the husband and wife. He is an extravert while she is an introvert.

Myers-Briggs Dichotomies

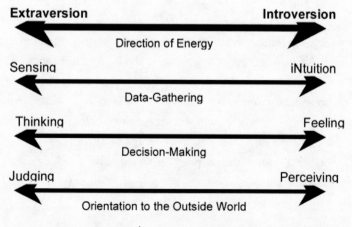

Most people typically consider the definition of extraversion as talkative and outgoing. If this is your understanding of extraversion, please let me change your definition of this misunderstood preference. Extraversion is the direction from which we get our energy. Extraverted people draw their energy from being with other people. Yes, in many cases, when extraverted people are in a group of people they are talking. However, when you put a group of extraverts in the same room, you will have some that are quiet while others are quite talkative.

I find myself in situations where I become reserved and fairly quiet. Business meetings where I am not leading the discussion and classes that I am not teaching are two situations where I tend to stay quiet and listen. Still, while I am quiet in some situations, I am a full-fledged extravert. I am also shy in most cases when I am around others that I don't know very well. I have to force myself to be more outgoing. However, my extraversion is evident; withdrawing from others will drain my energy and result in me needing my "batteries" recharged.

So how does one identify when someone is a real extravert? There are a several characteristics that can identify one as drawing energy from others or extraversion.

+ Extraverts speak to think.

+ Extraverts typically answer quickly even when the answer is not well thought out

+ Extraverts usually enjoy being more social than their counterparts.

+ Extraverts usually prefer to have many friends.

+ Extraverts usually become fatigued or stressed when they are spending a lot of time alone.

When I refer to someone who has a tendency to "speak to think" it does not mean that they cannot think when they are by themselves.

What it means is that a person can be stronger or at their best when thinking out loud or in a group of people. Extraverts will sometimes be talking when an idea hits them or when they are hear someone else mention something in the middle of a conversation. It is the free flow of conversation that can invigorate the extravert to deeper thinking and more creative ideas.

It is also a characteristic for an extravert to answer quickly or at least answer before they have thought through an idea and settled on an answer. What can be confusing for an introvert is that when the extravert spouts out an answer, it's not necessarily their final answer. Regis Philbin made the saying "Is that your final answer?" famous. When talking to the extravert, it can sometimes be necessary to ask this question in some fashion to come to a conclusion.

When my introverted wife asks me what I would like to do or what I would like to have, I will give her a quick answer. She assumes that I have thought it over deeply and considered all my options before giving the answer. That usually isn't the case. At the moment she asked, it was my *first* thought. However, given more options or more time to think about it, I may change my mind. That can be hard for her to understand at times since she prefers not to answer until given time to think through the situation. The challenge for us as a couple is when she holds me to my first answer (even if she would prefer me to change my mind) thinking that that is my preference.

To the introvert, the extravert can also appear flippant or "wishy washy," and unable to make a decision. Actually, the extravert can be just as good or as bad at decision-making as their introverted counterparts. What the introvert is seeing is their internal thought process occurring verbally. The extravert is usually just thinking out loud.

Social interactions can also be a characteristic of an extravert. Extraverts tend have a greater span of people they consider friends. Friendships of an extravert can be greater in breadth and sometimes less in depth than an introvert. Extraverts typically enjoy the social interactions with numbers of people. That doesn't mean they don't enjoy more intimate times with a few close friends. It is just that extraverts usually enjoy the larger gatherings more than introverts. Extraverts can play the room by bouncing from one person to the next; initiating conversation or listening intently.

The last characteristic we identified was the fatigue and stress increasing with the amount of time spent alone. Extraverts love their time alone and need it as much as anyone. What makes them differ from their counterparts is the need to extravert around others after a period of time. When extraverts spend a large block of time alone at work, they may be more exhausted by the end of the day than if they spent time with others intermittently. This is one reason more computer programmers or "tech heads" tend to be introverted rather than extraverted. Extraverts need the interaction to recharge.

In general, extraverts draw their energy from interactions with others and have their energy (mental and physical) drawn from them as they spend time alone. Conversely, the introvert can thrive on the very things that drain the extravert.

INTROVERT DOES NOT EQUAL SHY AND QUIET

When I first began a new position in a corporate training department, I was working closely with three men. Two of the men were quite loud, talkative, and funny to be around. They were the life of the party. The other appeared a little quieter than the others. Shortly after joining the group, I learned about the Myers-Briggs Type Indicator. One of my first revelations about the introversion preference was that the two talkative men in the department were actually introverts while the more reserved person was extraverted. Once I learned MBTI more intimately, I could easily see why these two were introverted even though they "seemed" to be extraverted.

The introverts had several characteristics that identified them as such, none of which were quiet and shy. The common characteristics for many introverts are as follows:

+   Introverts think to speak.

- Introverts may not be quick to respond on a new concept or idea.

- Introverts may not acknowledge hearing a comment for a period of time.

- Introverts tend to prefer fewer more intimate friends.

- Introverts tend to become fatigued and stressed when spending a lot of time with other people.

You can often identify a couple who are mixed in their preferences of introversion. The extravert will ask a question of their introverted partner. When the introvert doesn't answer immediately, the extravert will ask the question again or restate it as if it wasn't understood the first time.

Introverts typically prefer to think about their response before they comment. What can happen is that something is said and the introvert takes a moment to internally process the comment or question. They would rather not comment until they have thought through what they want to say. This is the reason for the delay in response. That is why we say that introverts think to speak. To accommodate the introvert, it is wise to ask a question or make a statement then count to ten. This allows the introvert to process what was said and formulate a response without being rushed.

One trait that is common among introverts is that when pressed for a quick answer, the answer is usually "no." I have learned over the years that if I spring something new on my wife, it works out much better if I tell her that I don't want an answer right away. She will go and think about it and come back to me much more agreeable than if I press for an immediate response.

Another behavior that springs up from the "think to speak" characteristic is a possible lack of acknowledgement about a comment made. When introverts engage in a conversation, it has been thought out quite extensively which means that assumptions have been made by the introverted person. When another person, whether introverted or extraverted, brings out a point that has not been internally processed, the reaction can appear to be a lack of acknowledgement that the comment was even heard. In fact, the comment may have been heard, but the introvert wants to internalize it before responding to it. It may even be days before the other person hears any acknowledgement on what was said. Here's a sample conversation to illustrate the point.

"Have you called Sara's teacher so we can discuss why her grades are down this year?" asked the introverted husband.

"Well, I've been thinking about that today," said the extroverted wife. "I know we've thought that with the extra language arts class she's taking, she has to work harder at her grades. But I was thinking it might be because two of her friends have moved away and she isn't quite as happy."

"Well, I would call right away so that we can talk with the teacher about what we can do to help her strengthen her language arts skills," he replied. "The teacher can let us know if we need to get her a tutor or something."

In this case, the wife is probably getting a little frustrated at this point. At no time did the introverted husband acknowledge that he even heard her comment about friends moving away. He went straight to the point they previously discussed. In fairness to the husband, the wife hasn't given him time to process the new idea, but on the other hand, the husband never acknowledged that he even heard what she had to say.

The lack of acknowledgement can be damaging to marriages. How many times do we hear, "you're not listening to me!" In some cases, it may be that the other person is listening, but has not had time to process the new information enough to make a rational comment. At some point, it is good for the introvert to acknowledge what was said and make a comment made toward the response. One way to do that is to paraphrase what was just said. A paraphrase is nothing more than repeating what you heard, but in your own words. A paraphrase doesn't agree or disagree; it just provides an acknowledgement that it was heard. In our example, a good paraphrase for the husband to add would be . . .

"So you think that it may not be the difficulty in the class. Instead, it may be that she is missing her old friends."

This lets the wife know that what she said was heard and important enough to be considered. The husband can also help the situation by letting his wife know that he would like to think about the new idea and let her know his opinion later. He could add, "Let me think about that." Remember, solid communication is the key to a good marriage.

Introverts not only communicate in a different way from the extravert, they also prefer to socialize in a different way. Their preference is generally to have fewer more intimate friends than the extravert. This does not mean that all introverts have deeper relationships than extraverts. What it does mean is that introverts feel more comfortable with a smaller gathering of friends rather than a larger party of people.

After a period of socialization, the introvert becomes fatigued and desires time alone to process and recharge his or her internal batteries. How long it takes before fatigue sets in is unique to each person, but in general the time is shorter with the introvert than the extravert. There are ways in which to find that time alone during socialization. A trip to the restroom can be a wonderful time alone in quiet solitude. For the introvert, the name of the room can bring new meaning. It truly becomes a room of rest.

Troy Simpson, an introverted friend and former co-worker of mine, gave me a wonderful expression of an introvert that I'll always remember. "Others see the introvert's second best," he said. What he meant was that when an introvert is at their best, they are internally processing for which others cannot see. What is visual to the outside world is not what the introvert does best.

STRATEGIES FOR CONFLICTING SPOUSES

In most cases, spouses do not have the same preferences in all the dichotomies. Marriages become stronger as the spouses learn about their differences and learn to cope with them by using effective strategies. When a couple understands each other's preferences and accepts them as God's gift of unique personalities, then coping skills develop more rapidly. Even more important is that one can understand their own personal needs and address them individually.

Coping skills work best when both parties in a marriage exercise compromise and enact personal strategies to meet their own needs. Each partner must work to understand the other's needs and *offer* ways for which their partner can express preferences. The following are some tips to help the process of fulfilling the needs of both partners in a marriage.

1. INTROVERTS NEED TIME TO INTERNALLY PROCESS THE DAY.

This can be especially challenging when the introverted individual is required to interact with people as a part of their job. He cannot just walk away from the interactions. Therefore, he becomes fatigued and somewhat stressed by the end of the day. As much as he loves his family, the last thing he needs is immediate interaction when he arrives home, unless he has had a long commute.

This can cause great conflict when his spouse is anxious to see him and he appears to want nothing to do with her. What usually happens is that one spouse pushes the other to interact. The result is that the introverted spouse works to get farther away from family to find the solitude he needs.

A female friend of mine experienced this each day. She couldn't understand why her husband would come home and rush out to mow the lawn or work on a hobby and basically ignore her and the kids. The problem was that he interacted with customers all day as part of his business. When the work-day ended, he had a five minute commute home which was not enough time to internally process and recharge. She would follow him around trying to converse with him. He would respond with nothing more than a few head nods and "um-humphs" to appear as if he was listening.

My suggestion to her was that she greet him when he arrives and then stay away from him for about thirty to forty-five minutes to allow him time to internally recharge. She initially balked at the idea. She claimed it took her a few hours to get him to talk to her as it was. If she delayed it more, he would be asleep before she could talk to him. I told her that if she would give him some time up front, she could have him the rest of the night.

Some time later, I asked my friend how it was working out. She was surprised at how much more willing he was to "really" listen and interact with her after she allowed him the time to rejuvenate himself.

2. EXTRAVERTS NEED INTERACTION TO INCREASE ENERGY.

A couple I know divorced after conflicts in preferences. One of contributing factors to the demise of the marriage was the extraverted husband's need to socialize after work and the introverted wife's desire to avoid it. This caused him to seek the interaction on his own. He began going alone since, when she did go, she was miserable and made that fact apparent to those around her. Rather than compromising, this couple went their own separate ways.

Some simple strategies can help a couple from escalating this conflict in preferences. To clear up possible assumptions, the extravert should not need to go out *every* night to socialize. Instead, interactions can occur in many forms during the day. If the extraverted spouse desires socialize every night, there may be other issues that need to be addressed. Occasional socializing mixed with normal everyday interactions should be sufficient for the extravert.

For the extravert who does not have much in the way of human interactions during the day, the challenge is to find ways to socialize. Lunch friends can go a long way in restoring his energy levels. Other "social" activities during the work day can include volunteering for committees or work teams on special projects. These activities require interaction to complete the job.

3. INTROVERTS NEED TIME TO THINK BEFORE GIVING AN ANSWER.

This statement isn't completely true. Introverts will give an answer to a new concept or idea, but the answer is usually "no." The typical introvert will prefer to spend some time internally processing the answer. Without that time to process, there is less risk involved by answering with "no."

To receive a more thought out response to a new concept or idea, it is better to ask the introvert in advance, and allow them time to process the answer. I have helped my introverted wife by asking her thoughts on an idea well before I need the answer. For example, I will call home during the day and ask her to think about new plans for the evening. She is generally more accepting of those ideas when she has time to think them through.

4. EXTRAVERTS NEED TO SPACE TO THINK OUT LOUD.

Many of the contestants on *Who Wants to be a Millionaire* will state a few possibilities for an answer. Regis Philbin would allow the contestants to speak for a moment to add to the suspense. In essence, the extraverted contestants were formulating their thoughts out loud. Then when it appeared that the contestant externally worked to the answer, Regis would ask the million-dollar question, "Is that your final answer?"

When speaking with an extraverted individual, it is sometimes wise to ask Regis' question or a similar question to pin down the final response. Extraverts need the time to externally process a response. However, it can be confusing to others who are not sure when the "real" response is finally mentioned. In many cases, this is where the married couple gets in the argument about what was previously said. It can go something like this.

"Why are you cooking Italian food? I thought you were going to cook a German dinner tonight?"

"Well, you said you wanted Italian!"

"I did not! Well, I did say that, but I changed my mind and said I wanted a German dinner instead."

"You say so many things, you confuse me."

To get a good response from the extraverted spouse, give your partner the space to think out loud and then pin him down with the question that forces them to make a final answer clear. "Is that your final answer?"

5. INTROVERTS PREFER TO HAVE A MORE INTIMATE SET OF FRIENDS RATHER THAN LARGE SOCIAL EVENTS.

I mentioned earlier about a couple who divorced after conflicts in socializing preferences. The extraverted husband wanted to go out with groups of friends. The introverted wife wanted to enjoy the quiet intimacy of her own home, and cringed at the thought of being out with groups of people.

Even though this point of socializing does not seem to be a sticking point that can lead to divorce, it can and does in many marriages. It often leads to an affair. The break in socializing together begins to separate the once inseparable couple. Once separated, each person in the relationship begins to drift into another direction. The spouse, whether man or woman, begins to find people that are more preferable to be around. This can include people from the opposite sex, which can lead to an affair.

The solution is compromise for differences in preferences. God put differing people together so that each one learns from the other. When one struggles, the other is there to pick him or her up.

> Two are better than one because they have good return for their labor. For if either of them falls, the one will lift up his companion. But woe to the one who falls when there is not another to lift him up. (Ecc. 4:9–10)

It is important for each person to compromise and learn coping strategies that enhance personal growth. God sometimes puts us in situations that are uncomfortable for us. His purpose is continued growth in our walk with him.

For an introvert who hates to socialize with large groups, there are a couple of options that make the socializing more tolerable. One way is to socialize with smaller groups of people whom you are more familiar—such as friends from work or from church will make the group more tolerable. In order to socialize in larger groups, find those groups that share common interests. If you are an animal lover, go to large events that focus on animals. If you have an affinity for restored cars, go to auto shows. Whatever the interest, there is a group out there that shares the same interest.

Some introverts prefer larger crowds at events so that they can be lost in the crowd and not be noticed. I had an introverted person tell me they loved going to a large church because the time of actual interaction was short and interaction was limited. Other such events with great numbers of people and limited interaction are professional sporting events and concerts.

Thus far, the strategies have been for couples doing things together. This is not to suggest that the couple must do everything together; each person may have different interests. Events such as men's night out or women's night out, works quite well in fulfilling socializing needs. Balance is the key to enhancing a relationship. Stronger marriages result from spending some time together and spending some time apart from one another.

Whatever type of social events introverts prefer, they cannot allow the extraverted partner to be the only one to suggest the types of socializing. The extravert will typically suggest a wider range of social events than would an introvert. To fulfill the need for interaction for the extravert, the introverted partner can take the lead and suggest events that he would find more acceptable. It will appease the need for interaction for the extravert while avoiding too much interaction for the introvert.

6. EXTRAVERTS MAY DESIRE MANY FRIENDS AND NOT LIMIT SOCIALIZING WITH THEM.

Over-socializing can lead the extraverted partner to find others who have similar preferences for socialization. When it comes to socializing without your spouse in groups that include those of the opposite sex, it is easy to find another partner that "understands" you, leading to an extra-marital affair.

To avoid problems that can come from filling your need for socializing with friends while making your spouse uncomfortable, the extravert should recognize the discomfort that may arise for their introverted spouse. Communication is the key. Talk with the introverted spouse to find out what types of socializing they prefer and work to accommodate it by finding and attending those events where they are more comfortable.

The more the couple compromises with the social calendar and the more they communicate their needs to one another, the less of a challenge the differences in their direction of energy become.

FAMOUS INTROVERTS AND EXTRAVERTS

One of my favorite extraverts is the Apostle Peter. He is the extravert's extravert. If Peter was thinking, his lips were moving. This caused him great joy at times and at other times it caused great grief. At one point, God even had to interrupt Peter to get a word in. Read the story of Jesus' transfiguration in chapter seventeen of the book of Matthew. There you will find Peter still speaking when a voice came from heaven.

Other famous extraverts include Lucille Ball and John Madden. John Madden, who is a color commentator for football broadcasts, makes the game more interesting with his comments. It seems like whatever he is thinking is coming out of his mouth. He makes a comment like, "Now this is football . . . there is mud and snow . . . it's cold . . . knuckles hurt when they hit a helmet. This is what it's all about." Nothing in this comment is well thought out. The words are excitable random thoughts of a man who is thinking out loud—to the pleasure of millions.

Famous Biblical introverts include Moses, David, and John. What is interesting about John is that he was with Peter while the Lord was transfiguring. In his case, you don't see anything written about him except that he was there. Why is that? Because being the introvert, John was internalizing this new event. His internal processing is not interactive; therefore there was no visual behavior to write about.

Some famous introverts include Adolph Hitler, John F. Kennedy, Johnny Carson, and Albert Einstein. It can be hard to imagine someone such as Adolph Hitler as an introvert. Even though he stood before so many to be seen and heard, he was still an introvert. However, Hitler may have spoken to many, but only a few close allies actually had conversations with him. He preferred to be with a select few on his hilltop retreat or indulging in his own thoughts.

As you can see, there are good and bad, successful and unsuccessful, in both categories of our dichotomy of introvert/extravert. It is time for you to assess yourself and determine which side of the dichotomy you reside on. Remember, you have to be one or another. You cannot be both. Yes, you will work on both sides of the dichotomy in differing parts of the day, but there is the natural person where you feel most comfortable.

Chapter 4

THE ORIENTATION TO THE OUTSIDE WORLD

Remember the romantic weekend trip I mentioned in chapter one? I planned a wonderful weekend in the bed and breakfast. I surprised my wife with the trip, and she hardly spoke for several hours.

Why did the romantic weekend start off so rocky and unromantic? It was my failure to understand the real needs of my wife rather than the societal norms that dictate what a wife should like. So often we rely on what society deems typical behavior and response. Man plans a romantic weekend trip, wife melts into a puddle of goo and follows husband faithfully. Well, that is the equation, but it doesn't always work that way.

For us, and many others, this kind of problem is the differences in our individual Orientation to the Outside World.

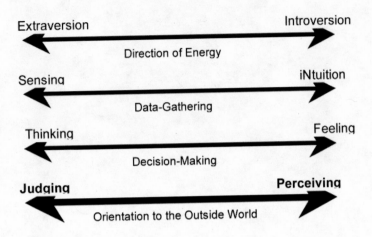

Myers-Briggs Dichotomies

Extraversion ←————————————————→ Introversion
Direction of Energy

Sensing ←————————————————→ iNtuition
Data-Gathering

Thinking ←————————————————→ Feeling
Decision-Making

Judging ←————————————————→ **Perceiving**
Orientation to the Outside World

STRUCTURED AND ORGANIZED VERSUS SPONTANEOUS

This dichotomy has the structured, planned, and organized preferences on one side and the spontaneous on the other side. In the previous story, my wife takes the planning side of the dichotomy. She had her Friday planned. Not only was it planned, but it was already planned by Wednesday. On the other hand, I am the more spontaneous.

You may be thinking that I am a planner since I planned the weekend. I did make a plan, but as usual, my plans are loose and have more flexibility to them. I had not planned a time to arrive. I had no plans for where we would eat or what we would do. All I planned was to take the day off, make reservations in advance, and make provisions for the care of our daughter. Those three plans were necessary to make the trip. The rest of the trip was an adventure into the unknown, and I was ready to decide what to do and where to go when I arrived.

My mistake was that I did not take into consideration my wife's preferences of planning and control. She lost control of the plan and was forced to be spontaneous. This gave her a feeling of stress since she was unable to plan for anything. She did not know where we were staying, nor did she know what we would be doing over the next two days. She didn't even know what direction we would be traveling.

Now many of you are thinking how stressful that situation would be for you. Remember, my wife is also introverted. This means she now must turn inward to sort out in her mind what is happening in the situation. That is why she was not talking to me. In fact, she spent most of the time not really hearing me when I was talking, since she was forced by me to turn inward. The reason she couldn't work through it for so long was that although she was sorting it out in her mind, she had no information to sort. If she had some of the information like destination or itinerary, she would have been able to process the information and move on.

I, on the other hand, was excited about the trip. I didn't know what we were going to do or where we were going to eat. I had never been to this little town and knew nothing of what it offered. The only determinant to choosing this town was that it had a historic bed and breakfast. Regina had always wanted to stay at a bed and breakfast, so that was going to be part of the surprise.

I was energized by the adventure of finding a good restaurant where I had never eaten before. I enjoyed the search for the sites of interest in the area. The thought of just going and figuring out what to do and where to go on the fly adds interest to the trip. In fact, too much planning for a trip seems to take all the fun out of it for me.

The differences in our preferences of orientation to the outside world are called Judging and Perceiving. Typically, the title of judging invokes strong feelings of an anti-Christian behavior. However, judging has nothing to do with one person judging another. Judging in this reference is only a name given to those who prefer a planning approach to life.

JUDGING DOES NOT MEAN "ONE WHO JUDGES OTHERS"

Judgers are oriented to the outside world through planning and organizing. They love to be prepared for the day by having a set plan, especially if the plan is prepared the previous day. Judgers also like to have events planned in advance. Whether it's a night out on the town or a vacation, there is comfort in having a plan for the event.

One of the favorite tools for planning and organizing is the list. The list is used for organizing events of the day, what to buy at the store, or even what to watch on TV. Lists can take on many forms, depending on the person or the need for the list. In fact, lists don't even need to be written down, they can be mental lists. Regardless of the form, planning and listing are key indicators of a preference of judging.

When making the list, judgers prefer to make them with a certain structure. I have found most judgers prefer to make their to-do list with each item listed in one of two ways. The list is made by order of importance or by order in which they are to be accomplished. In this case, the first item on the list would be the first to complete, the second item on the list is the second task to complete, and so on.

One of the greatest pleasures for the judger is to checkmark an item on the list when the task is completed. What makes the checkmark more pleasurable is when it is made in order. As I mentioned earlier, the list is preferred to be made in the order for which the items should be completed. So when an item is checked out of order, it still feels good, but not as good as it could have if the items checked were in the listed order.

When my wife told me of her plans for that fateful Friday, she mentioned the tasks in the order for which she planned to complete them. There was meaning to why each one was listed in order. She planned to go shopping at the mall. Her second stop was to the bank to handle a transaction because the bank was next to the mall. She planned to finish the day with grocery shopping since there would be refrigerated items that shouldn't sit in a warm car while she did other things.

What brings stress for the judger is when someone or something disrupts planned activities. Even if the disruption is something the judger prefers over the current plan, there is some stress that results from a sudden change in the plan.

There are more characteristics to identify one who prefers the judging preference than just making lists. The following is a list of some of the judger's characteristics with regard to orientation to the outside world:

- Preferences of the judger are typically that he or she . . .

- Likes to make lists, whether written or mental, in priority order.

- Likes to check off completed items on the list from top to bottom.

- Prefers to plan rather than act spontaneously.

- Becomes stressed when the unplanned event disrupts the plan.

- Prefers to work steadily on one thing until it is completed rather than multi-task.

- Prefers rules and regulations to give organization and structure.

- Feels that they are spontaneous when they plan to be spontaneous at a certain time.

Rather than acting on a whim, those with a judging preference prefer to plan their actions. A plan can consist of a formal written set of actions or can be a simple as thoughts as to how to move forward to complete a process. Judgers can work out things spontaneously, but again, it can cause some stress. The comfort comes with having a plan in place to make things happen.

This was extremely evident as I moved into a new home during the writing of this chapter. There were a number of large cartons destined for the kitchen sitting on counters and on the kitchen floor. My wife was going to tackle the placing of the dishes, cups, saucers, glasses, food, and so on. My wonderful mother-in-law (yes, you read that correctly. I don't look at her as a mother-in-law, I see her more as a friend) was there to help my wife put these box loads of goods into the cabinets. As my wife put it, "I couldn't have done it without her."

The reason it wouldn't have been done was because my wife wanted to plan how everything should go before she started with the first box. She would have had to decide what items she had, and determined where they would be best placed. For example, she would have thought out how she cooks and what items she would reach for the most. She would have to determine in what order she would fill the cabinets, which would determine the cartons to be opened first.

On the other hand, my mother-in-law just began to open boxes and placing items where she thought they should go. My wife, knowing what was happening, decided to jump in and follow her mother for periods of time. Although she could do it when push came to shove, she did not prefer to act without a plan. To relieve the stress of this situation, she would leave the kitchen for periods of time to vacuum a floor or dust a shelf in a closet. This allowed her to recover somewhat and enter back into the kitchen to work.

When a plan is made for the judger, any disruption to the plan causes a little frustration or stress. This can happen even when the disruption is a good one. For example, a man with a judging preference plans to mow the lawn and clean the garage on Saturday. Sunday he plans to go to church and balance the checkbook. On Saturday morning, a friend calls and tells him that he has two tickets to watch the Cubs game at Wrigley Field. Although his favorite summertime interest is the Cubs, his first thought is, *Well, I planned to mow the lawn and clean the garage.* He is stressed and quickly thinks of how to rearrange (or re-plan) the day. *I can mow the lawn quickly, shower, and then go to the game. I will be home about five in the afternoon, so I can eat supper and clean the garage that evening.* "Sure, I can go."

Another problem arises for our judger. It turns out to be one of the best games of the year as the Cubs come from behind and tie the game in the ninth inning. Although he is excited about the game, there is a thought that keeps haunting him. He notices that he will get home later than planned and is really rooting for a quick end to the game so he can finish his plan.

There is a comfort level in a plan working out as planned, even when the change in the plan is enjoyable. Most plans for a person with judging preference are to work on one thing at a time and completing it before moving on to the next task. Again, this became evident during our move while writing this chapter.

I had unloaded a number of boxes into our new home. It seemed like there were so many cartons that it was getting difficult to walk around the house. It was especially difficult in the kitchen, where boxes were stacked on counters and floors just ready to be opened and placed in shelves. My suggestion for my judging wife was to begin emptying the boxes and putting the goods into the cabinets, while I continued to unload cartons. Her preference was for everyone to continue unloading cartons until that task was completed. She could check "unload cartons" off the mental list and move on to the next mental note on the list. It took a couple of urgings from me, but she gave in as she understood my reasons. The purpose for me was that the elimination of some boxes would give me room to bring more stuff in the house. It wasn't her first choice though, since her preference is to complete one task before beginning another.

Another comfort zone for the typical person with judging preference is working under the structure of rules and regulations. Although most judgers would not like to have too many rules and regulations that restrict real freedoms, they do like more guidance to the "dos" and "don'ts" than their counterparts with a perceiving preference.

This conflict of preferences comes to light quickly in church organizations. For example, when it is determined that the dress in the congregation is becoming a little too revealing, we tend to make rules to determine what is appropriate. We, as a church, will add a rule of "modest length of skirts" and determine exact number of inches below the knee or above the floor the dress must come. Then comes the school marm out with her ruler to measure and determine if the young lady's skirt is one half inch too short. Although I mention this in jest, when judging leadership gets too comfortable with an abundance of rules, the intent becomes forgotten and the rule becomes the focal point.

I supervised a woman who had a small child and was at the breaking point both emotionally and financially as her husband ran out on her. She could barely afford clothes for herself and her baby. She did not have a relationship with the Lord and spoke to me about finding Jesus. Bound by more rules, I was limited as to what I could say and do since she was my employee. The church I attended was over an hour away, and she had no car. I suggested that she attend a church in the small town where we worked.

The Monday after she attended her first church service, she was bubbling over with excitement. She was glad that she took the time to attend the service close to her home. She spoke of attending the next Sunday and even considered giving her heart to the Lord. The bubble quickly burst as a lay leader in the church, who was another employee, asked her not to attend the services any more until she could "dress like a woman" (wear a dress). I'm not saying that it is wrong for a believer to believe that women should wear dresses, but I am saying that we sometimes allow rules to supersede God's work. Remember, this woman was dirt poor and never attended church prior to that fateful Sunday. She didn't even own a dress at the time. The woman was so hurt, she never attempted to return to another church. The last time I saw her, she still had no relationship with the Lord or even a desire to have one. In this case, the rule overshadowed the purpose of the church to reach the lost for Christ.

Keep in mind that the law was given to Israel so that sin would increase. Paul wrote in the letter to the Romans:

> *The Law came in so that the transgression would increase; but where sin increased, grace abounded all the more.* (Romans 5:20)

Can we enact so many rules that we actually increase sin? Yes, we can put so many rules in place that no one can measure up. This poor woman who couldn't afford a dress was pushed away by the rules that declared she didn't measure up to worship with the church.

However, rules are necessary. Even the most ardent perceiver will admit to needing some rules. They get out of hand when they take away all the decision-making power of the individual and stifle the work of God.

The last characteristic mentioned above for the judger is the preference for planning spontaneity. When teaching Myers-Briggs basics in business, I often have participants come to me at a break and tell me they fall into the judging category, but they consider themselves to be spontaneous. When I question them to get a sense for how spontaneous they are, I get responses that go something like this: "Every Saturday I make sure I don't plan anything so I can do whatever." If the day of spontaneity is determined in advance, it is not spontaneous.

PERCEIVING DOES NOT MEAN PERCEPTIVE

The individuals who prefer spontaneity and less structure are the perceivers, who can be highly misunderstood by their judging partners. In fact, in a typical Myers-Briggs class with couples, I have a judging spouse that wants to "fix" their perceiving spouse by getting them involved in lists and plans. Judgers, I am sorry to say, that although lists and plans work very well for you, they can actually be limiting or counterproductive to the perceiver.

The perceiver works in a different realm of activity from the judger. Living for the moment and having a number of options is the preference for these people. Their joy is the adventure of life with open options and an undetermined plan of action, or at least a modicum of a plan. Although they can work very well under a plan, perceivers prefer plans that are somewhat flexible and allow some creativity. Here are the general characteristics of the perceiver:

+ Prefers to act spontaneously rather than to adhere to a strict plan or a routine.

+ Likes only enough structure to allow for flexibility and creativity.

- Can become energized when the unplanned event disrupts the plan.
- Can become bored when working on one thing for too long and prefers to multi-task.

Judgers, who love to plan, will sometimes think that perceivers never plan or never adhere to a plan. This couldn't be further from the truth. Perceivers do create some wonderful plans and do it on a regular basis. However, the perceiver's plan looks quite different from the judger's plan.

The plans that perceivers make will look more loosely developed and contain options that allow the perceiver to choose a course of action depending on the circumstance. For example, the plans for a perceiver's evening may be: mow the lawn unless it rains, then clean the garage. In this case, there is little thought to exact timing for the event, and there is an option. Will the perceiver eat in this case? Sure, it was unplanned, but dinner is a given and has no need to be planned. Besides, the perceiver doesn't really want to decide on dinner until he has determined what he is in the mood to eat.

While teaching a class on Myers-Briggs in Oklahoma, I had a woman in the class ask me how I function on the weekends without planning them ahead of time. She explained that she and her judging husband could not even decide what restaurant they should eat at unless they planned days ahead of time. My response was that they could miss out since the decision was made before they knew what they would have a taste for on that particular day. She responded that they work themselves into the mood for the certain restaurant by planning for it. Thus you have the difference in planning. The perceiver may plan to go out to eat ahead of time, but there is an option to the plans based on the mood for the day.

Although the perceiver likes the spontaneity of living for the moment, they do not necessarily like chaos. Some structure fits a perceiver just fine. In fact, many perceivers need some structure to keep them on track. But, when structure stifles any flexibility and creativity, the perceiver may tend to rebel.

The last two characteristics mentioned are on polar opposites. They are the boredom that comes with routine and the energizing that comes from an unplanned event. Those with a perceiving preference may live and work in routines for the most part. Routines are impossible to avoid. However, the monotony of routine can bring fatigue and stress to most perceivers. They look forward to the disruption of a routine day.

The strength of a perceiver can be the ability to meet an unplanned crisis situation. As a teenager and a perceiver, I stood in the kitchen of our East Nashville home when my mother and I heard two loud "booms." I ran outside to find the first bang was a car jumping a curb and striking a local teen in the back, throwing him about one hundred feet into the second story of the home behind us. The second bang was the uncontrolled car breaking through the brick wall of the basement, barely missing the youth.

Neighbors joined me in running out to aid the victim. As I got to the scene, I noticed people shouting to one another to get the injured youth in the house and call 911. Most of them were panicked and shouting instructions, but no one was doing anything. I quickly cautioned that if he was moved, there was a good chance we could paralyze him if he wasn't already.

I designated one person to call 911, then sent a couple of younger people to get blankets so we could treat him for shock. I had a couple of others hold the teen in case he tried to move, so he wouldn't do any more damage than was already done to his body.

Was I the hero? No. I really didn't do much of anything. All that I did was use my energy from the break in the routine to organize everyone into doing what they were taught to do. According to the doctors, those who stabilized him and treated him for shock before the medics arrived prevented his broken back from severing the spinal cord. A few months later, the youth who was struck could be seen walking down the neighborhood sidewalks.

Not only can perceivers become energized by the unplanned, they can become bored with the routine. It's not that perceivers don't follow a routine, they do, it's just that perceivers become bored with the routine over time and welcome the relief of a break in the routine. If no break occurs for a long period of time, the perceiver will tend to make their own breaks.

STRATEGIES FOR CONFLICTING COUPLES

Once again, there is an opportunity to learn more about yourself and your spouse's needs. Armed with the knowledge and understanding this brings, we can look at the strategies each of you can use to cope with the differences in preference with respect to the orientation to the outside world.

I. JUDGERS PREFER TO USE LISTS AND PLANS TO ORGANIZE.

Judgers love to organize their thoughts, time, and events that shape their day. Lists are a wonderful tool that a judger uses to organize. The preference is to build the list in a way that it can be worked from top to bottom, checking off each one as it is completed before moving to the next item. Deviation from this can be burdensome for the spouse of the judger, because they may not see the list in the same perspective as the person who authored the list.

Whether the spouse of the list-maker is judger or perceiver, there is a possibility of treating the list as it was written. This is primarily due to a differing values system or preference of type. If the author of the list views the spouse as deviating from the plan, frustration can occur.

Communication of expectations can be a key to understanding. Judgers who create a list or plan can realize others may have another way of doing things. In addition, they must come to grips with the fact that the order of priority items on the list isn't always the best or only order of priority in which to create a list. Proverbs chapter 16 tells us that the ways of man are right in their own eyes. Communicating why things are on the list in the order which they were written can help both parties in a marriage.

2. PERCEIVERS NEED THE FREEDOM FOR OPTIONS IN A PLAN.

Lists are a great organizer, and the judger loves to use them. Contrary to what you may think, perceivers don't hate lists; they can work with or without them. The challenge for the perceiver is when the lists stifle them and limit their options.

To minimize the impact, the judger can develop lists with the notion that the perceiver will look at the list differently. The perceiver won't necessarily attempt to work the list from top to bottom. They may choose an item out of the middle to deal with first. In addition, the perceiver may work on more than one item on the list at a time. The judgers need to understand that, though they may perform more efficiently working on one thing at a time, perceivers may actually be less effective. Perceivers have the knack of performing some things very effectively when not focusing on one thing at a time. Boredom can actually slow the progress of the perceiver who is forced to focus on only one thing at a time for a long period of time.

3. JUDGERS ARE MORE COMFORTABLE WITH A PLAN.

Living spontaneously stresses the judger. When they enter the weekend without a plan or go on a vacation that is not at least somewhat planned, they may not have the full enjoyment they expect. Compromising on how spontaneous planned events are can make the time together for judgers and perceivers much more enjoyable and less stressful.

Since judgers like plans and perceivers like options, the conflicting preferences can be met by making loose plans or plans that have built-in decision points. In other words, make a plan that has certain points where the perceiver has the option to choose going one way or another. This allows the judger to have a plan and the perceiver to not feel as if they have had all their options taken away. For example, in planning a date for Saturday night a couple can plan to go out to eat and take in a movie. Options can be left open as to which order the two events happen depending on how hungry the couple are. There is also the option as to what movie they will see. The mood of the couple can be for a drama, comedy, or action picture depending on how the day went for the two of them. Allowing the judger to plan loosely and allowing the perceiver to choose the option that fits best for the moment can make for a more enjoyable and less confrontational evening.

4. PERCEIVERS FAVOR FEWER RULES AND REGULATIONS.

Too many house rules on how everything is to be done can be stifling and stressful to the perceiver. On the other hand, the judger may feel a little stress if the home has no order as to how things are handled.

The couple of differing preferences should look at having some order to the home, but not so much that it stresses the perceiver. One way to develop a compromise is to look at the areas that are most important to each person, and allow that person to either develop the order and rules, or allow the person to leave it less in order. For example, if the wife or husband enjoys doing things in the garage and the spouse does not, then allow the one who enjoys working in the garage the option to keep it ultra organized or somewhat disorganized or seemingly out of sorts. However, the spouse should pick their "space" and be able to organize it or leave it flexible as they choose.

The key to making this work is that the other person must honor how their spouse chooses to utilize their space. If one person chooses the hobby room as their space to keep less than ultra-organized, the spouse should honor that request and not sneak in the room to clean and organize it without permission.

Again, successful strategies in living a harmonious marriage rely on each person in the marriage to recognize and allow for some of their preferences to be practiced.

Although behavior is not a complete picture of someone's type, we can see some tendencies and make some assumptions as to the probable type of some historical figures. It can be eye opening to view some of the personalities in the Bible and attempt to figure out whether they were judgers or perceivers.

One of the classic cases of a judger in my mind is Moses. Here is a man who worked best when things are organized and struggled when things were disorganized. As a man who had a judging preference, he had been gifted to work best under highly structured rules and regulations. No one knows the mind of God, but it seems quite evident that God directed a man who was gifted with judging to deliver a new set of standards to the nation of Israel in the form of the Ten Commandments.

Other famous judgers include Presidents John F. Kennedy, Richard Nixon, and Franklin D. Roosevelt as well as Sam Walton of Walmart fame.

At least one expert on Myers-Briggs lists Simon Peter with a judging preference. However, I disagree with this opinion. The Apostle Peter was on the other end of the dichotomy from Moses. He was able to adapt very well to new situations with his flexibility and preference for spontaneity. This was evident in his increased energy level when faced with an unplanned situation, such as when he witnessed Jesus transfiguring and again when Jesus was arrested.

Other famous perceivers include Presidents John Adams and Teddy Roosevelt as well as Albert Einstein.

Again, a variety of heroes and villains can be found on both sides of the preference dichotomy of the orientation to the outside world. Consider your own tendencies as to which side of the dichotomy you feel most comfortable. Are you the kind of person who leans more toward structure, organization, and lists, or are you the kind of person who tends to be more spontaneous and flexible?

Chapter 5

THE DATA-GATHERING FUNCTION

"We were in Virginia last week when we stopped at a little country church," said Sam, the outgoing gentleman in my Sunday school class.

"No, it wasn't Virginia, it was North Carolina," interrupted his wife Jan.

"Well, we were in North Carolina last week," he continued.

"That wasn't last week. Last week you had to go to the doctor's for tests," she interrupted again. "We were in North Carolina two weeks ago."

"Okay, we were in North Carolina two weeks ago when we visited this little country church. For a Wednesday night service it looked to have a good crowd."

She interrupted again, "It was a Sunday night, not Wednesday night and they told us it was a normal size crowd."

Finally, the man, showing some frustration at not getting to tell his story looked straight at his wife and said, "All that doesn't matter. It has nothing to do with the point I'm trying to make."

"The story doesn't make sense if you don't get it right," she replied.

Ignoring his wife, he continued with his story. "What I wanted to tell you is that we met a couple while we were at this church. It turns out that we knew them when we all lived in Texas years ago. They were quite a wild couple and never went to church, but we continue to pray for them after we moved out of Texas. It was quite a thrill for us to have

God put us in the same church, hundreds of miles away, to let us know how they were doing."

Although the class was amazed at the story, most of them were internally wondering why there was so much debate on the details of the story, when in fact, it really didn't have relevance to the point of the story. This is a classic example of the difference in preference of our next dichotomy—the data-gathering function.

THE CONCRETE VERSUS THE NEVER-ENDING POSSIBILITIES

The irritation with this couple stemmed from their differing preference in gathering information. For the wife, the validity of a story or idea is in the concrete facts that surround it. For the husband, the importance in the story is the overall idea or the point of the story makes, with the details being pointless. He probably feels that the details can get in the way of a good story or idea.

The conflict with this couple lies within the dichotomy of data-gathering. This internal function is not always as easy to spot as whether a person is structured or spontaneous, but it can lead to some irritation for a couple when not understood.

The data-gathering function deals with how a person collects information. We generally take in information through the five senses of seeing, hearing, smelling, tasting, and feeling.

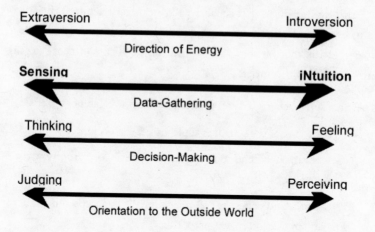

Myers-Briggs Dichotomies

Extraversion ←——————————————→ Introversion
Direction of Energy

Sensing ←——————————————→ **iNtuition**
Data-Gathering

Thinking ←——————————————→ Feeling
Decision-Making

Judging ←——————————————→ Perceiving
Orientation to the Outside World

On one side of this dichotomy we have those who prefer sensing. Sensors prefer focusing on the present. They like to deal with concrete facts and data. On the other side of the dichotomy are those who prefer intuition, or those who function more with ideas, concepts, and possibilities. They typically look toward the future and how things could be. Theories are more interesting to the intuitive than the sensor.

In our story, the wife prefers sensing. The importance of the story loses some relevance when it is convoluted with facts that are not completely true. To her, the story loses credibility when the occurrence is a week off, or if the state is incorrect. For the intuitive husband in the story, it really doesn't matter whether the state is North Carolina or Virginia. The fact that it was hundreds of miles from Texas and the idea that God brought the couple together was what was important to him.

SENSING THE CONCRETE FACTS THAT SURROUND US

The data-gathering dichotomy is based on one becoming aware of the things or events that surround us. The sensing function hones in on what surrounds the person through observation of the senses. In other words, the sensors are more in tune with the details of the surroundings.

This doesn't mean that sensors will catch every detail of their surroundings and intuitives will miss every detail around them. What it does mean is that sensors have a tendency to focus on those details more so than the intuitive.

There are several characteristics that can indicate a preference of sensing:

- The focus of the sensor is typically on the present.

- Accurate facts tend to become more of the focus than the concepts or ideas they represent.

- Theories and concepts are more difficult to accept, unless there is an application that is practical.

An example of this may be how the sensor looks at what a wonderful day it is today. *The temperature is 78 degrees with low humidity. The wind is out of the south at less than 10 miles per hour, making it even more comfortable. The sky is clear with only a few cumulus clouds here and there. It's peaceful enough that you can hear the sounds of mourning doves lining up on the telephone lines.*

Notice the detail that is in the description of what makes the day wonderful. The facts are accurate to the best of the sensor's knowledge with solid detail on why the day is truly marvelous. The focus is on the experience at the moment. When coupled with the perceiving attitudes, sensor's living for the moment can be enhanced to the point of irritation to others. There is an excitement with experiencing the moment to the fullest and worrying about the consequences of their actions after the moment.

This is in contrast to the intuitive who may experience the same thing and relate it in a different way. *What a beautiful day. Warm air with gentle breezes kisses my face. Sounds of birds fill a cloudless sky. The day holds a potpourri of things to do.*

We will discuss the intuitive side characteristics later in the chapter. What is important here is to notice the lack of specifics and the potential for the rest of the day.

Since the focus is on the sensory perception of the world surrounding the sensor, there is an importance with the accuracy of the details around a subject or event. That is why the wife in the story was not content with the relating of the story by her husband. He was describing an event that was different than what she experienced.

Validity of facts is important to the sensor. Where the sensor tends to struggle is with vague concepts or theories with little practical application. A sensor reading this book and learning about the theory of personality type will have trouble understanding or accepting it without some information that makes it practical and relative to everyday life. Once the sensor sees information that makes it practical in his life, personality type becomes relevant to him.

INTUITIVE INSIGHT OF POSSIBILITIES, MEANINGS, AND RELATIONSHIPS

Characteristics that can indicate a preference for intuition are:

- The focus of the intuitive can be directed toward the future potential.

- A concept, theory, or idea is the focus of the intuitive rather than the specifics, details, or facts.

- Theories, concepts, and ideas are invigorating for the intuitive.

- Intuitives can be more readily attuned to symbolisms of things and events.

What a beautiful day. Warm air with gentle breezes kisses my face. Sounds of birds fill a cloudless sky. The day holds a potpourri of things to do.

Notice that there is little in the way of facts to describe the day. Most of our intuitive statement is based on the concept of a beautiful day that is relative to the opinion of the originator of the statement. It may be a great day for that person, but the air temperature can vary from the sixties to the nineties. The sounds of the birds may not be as enjoyable for many. The intuitive doesn't give detail to what kind of birds are singing. Mourning doves were described in the sensor statement. Since it is mourning doves, I can assure you that my mother, if she were still alive, would not appreciate the sound. To her, mourning doves give a mournful sound that can be depressing to hear.

What is important to the intuitive is the concept of a wonderful day. The vague description is perfect for the intuitive, who can use his own concept of wonderful, and create in his mind the perfect day.

Notice also, the focus of the statement. It ends with the potential for the future. The intuitive relishes the potential to do many things before having to make the decision as to what really needs to be accomplished. This is in stark contrast to the sensor and his focus on the present.

Two other characteristics highlight the intuitive preference. The first one is the tendency to focus on the concepts or big picture with less focus on the details. The second characteristic is the preference for symbolism of things and events.

When intuitives focus on the big picture, they are looking for the best method or situation for a process. For example, my father-in-law is always looking at the big picture of life. He lives each day looking for opportunities to solidify his retirement. Every purchase he makes, every project he undertakes, every career decision is predicated on how well it will position him for retirement. Though most sensors will make some choices that are advantageous for retirement, they do not have the same big picture obsession as my father-in-law. For with him, there are missed present-day opportunities, because they have no relevance to the over-all view of the impending retirement.

The other preference mentioned is the tendency toward symbolism. Intuitives more naturally view things using symbolism. Sensors and intuitives alike can see symbolism in obvious objects such as the American flag. However, it is the intuitive that tends to see more symbolism in the not-so-symbolic objects and events: A new initiative at work is a symbol of the changing values within a company; a wise decision by a teenager is a symbol of maturity in decision-making; a vote for a certain candidate is a sign of the changing dynamics in the local population base. Symbolism is the lens with which intuitives view the world.

STRATEGIES TO ADDRESS DIFFERENCES IN DATA-GATHERING

The data-gathering function of sensing and intuition is not the most challenging of the four dichotomies in a marriage setting. However, there can be some irritation that arises because of the differences in the data-gathering process. Therefore, we have a couple of strategies to minimize the impact of differences in this dichotomy.

I. SENSORS SHOULD CONVEY AN OVERALL CONCEPT BEFORE SHARING DETAILS.

With sensors, concrete and accurate facts and details are the foundation for any good plan or idea. It can be so important to the sensor that they forget to convey the idea or concept before diving into the details. This is difficult for any spouse, but it is especially difficult for the intuitive spouse to endure. He is hit with a menagerie of details without understanding the purpose for it. It is like being told the recipe for a dish before knowing what it is we are cooking and what we are cooking it for.

To make the detail easier to swallow for the spouse, conversation should be directed to the overall idea before diving into details. In other words, get to the point first. Then add some details as needed to help the other person understand. Remember, the point in conversation is to convey an understanding, not inundate them with unnecessary dribble.

It may sound harsh, but if you are a person that likes to rattle off a lot of information about anything, remember what it is like for you to listen to a salesperson rattle on long after you already decided to make the purchase.

2. INTUITIVES SHOULD CONSIDER ADDING SOME DETAIL FOR THE SENSOR.

Those who have a preference of intuition, can sometimes be so enthralled with an idea that they ignore the need for other's need to know some of the details. The feeling is that the idea is so good that everyone should just fall over in excitement and buy into it, without hearing any of the details. Sometimes the intuitive can even be irritated and almost offended that his spouse doesn't share his same excitement for an idea.

The one with the intuitive preference can enhance the acceptance of an idea by their sensing spouse with less irritation by providing some details. This allows the sensor spouse to accept the validity of the idea with the concrete foundation of solid details.

FAMOUS SENSORS AND INTUITIVES

Although this dichotomy does not produce as much outward indication of preference as the attitudes, we can still see evidence of the preference toward sensing or intuition.

John seems to win the award for the clearest intuitive in the Bible. With his focus on symbolism that was inspired during his time on the island of Patmos, he writes the book of Revelations. This book is rich with symbolism. He writes of seven churches that many currently refer to as the current church. Some look at the seven churches as the time-line of the church. Revelations is also rich with animals that represent certain people, groups, or beings.

John also shows evidence of his intuition in the Gospel of John. The book begins with a play on words which is typically associated with those of intuitional preference:

In the beginning was the Word, and the Word was with God, and the Word was God. (John 1:1)

Words are basically symbols with certain meanings. Those who like to wordsmith or make a play on words usually have a bent for intuition. Other intuitives in the Bible can be found in the Old Testament. David is one who shows a preference toward intuition with his writings in the Psalms. The deeply symbolic poetry is a testament to his faithfulness in God Almighty. Other books rich with symbolism are the book of Daniel and the book of Ezekiel.

Those in the Bible who lean toward the other side of the data-gathering dichotomy include Moses and Peter. Moses' attention to the detail made him a perfect choice to focus on the law of God. His sensing coupled with the judging preference, provides him with a heightened preference for rules, laws, and regulations. Peter on the other hand, shows his bent for sensing, coupled with his perceiving, in his constant air of living for the moment. Peter often acted first, and then learned of the consequences of his actions after the fact. This is evident in the story of the cock crowing. He was quick to say that he would never deny Jesus, but when the moment came, he seized the opportunity that looked best in the short term.

Other famous non-Biblical sensors include Harry Truman, Lyndon Johnson, and Steve Spurrier. Again, a variety of heroes and villains can be found on both sides of the preference dichotomy of the Data Gathering. Consider your own tendencies as to which side of the dichotomy you feel most comfortable. Are you the type of person who focuses on concrete facts and details, or do you feel more comfortable with new ideas, concepts, and theories?

Chapter 6

THE DECISION-MAKING FUNCTION

"Angela" was my administrative assistant for a couple of years. Angela and her husband, "Jack" filled out an MBTI and verified the findings with me. In order to maximize the strength of their relationship, Angela consistently discussed with me the dynamics of type in their marriage.

One day, Angela came into my office somewhat frustrated with a situation involving her car breaking down on a regular basis. The frustration arose from the difference in opinion on what the couple should do with the car.

In the most recent event, Angela's car broke down in a mall parking lot after dark. Prior to that, she had been stranded on the side of the road a few times. In each case, Jack came quickly to her rescue. Waiting for Jack was a nerve-racking experience for Angela, as she felt vulnerable stranded alone. Not only was fear devastating during the wait, but there was a constant stress that welled up within her every time she was in her car. She never knew when the next break down would occur. Angela felt that purchasing another vehicle would solve the problem.

Jack, on the other hand, was very adept to financial concepts. He followed concepts that would help the couple achieve financial security for years to come. He determined that buying another car at that time was not the financially sound thing to do. The repairs to the car would cost less than buying good quality used vehicle. He never had a problem with reaching Angela when she was stranded or paying for repairs that he couldn't be perform himself. Jack felt that now was just not the right time to purchase another vehicle from a logical financial viewpoint.

Angela understood the logic behind Jack's opinion and she appreciated him for his knowledge of finances. What frustrated her was that there was another component that Jack's logic did not take into consideration: the impact of the situation on the person most affected, in this case, his wife. The other issue was her desire for the whole situation to be over without her having to face conflict with Jack.

This conflict is a classic situation centering in the realm of our last function called decision-making.

LOGIC VERSUS THE IMPACT ON PEOPLE

As you can imagine from the name, this function deals with the way in which we make decisions each day. After we gather the information through sensing or intuition, we make decisions from the information we retain. The impact of decisions does not have to be large. In fact, most of our decisions can be rather insignificant. They can be as simple as what to eat or who to call on the phone.

On one side of the decision-making function is Angela, who has a preference we refer to as "feeling." On the other side is Jack, who has a preference that we refer to as "thinking." The difference in their opinion regarding the car situation is the perspective from which they initially begin the decision-making process. As you can imagine, Angela's feeling preference causes her to focus on the impact on people. She realizes that financially, buying another vehicle isn't the best idea, but from a safety standpoint (especially her own) purchasing another car is the best option. Jack's thinking preference causes him to focus on the logical financial issues.

Myers-Briggs Dichotomies

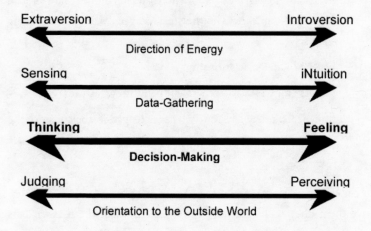

In fairness to Jack, he doesn't necessarily view the situation as a safety hazard as quickly as Angela does. From his logical viewpoint, he sees a safe remedy in her having a cell phone, and his willingness to respond immediately while she is in the safety of a locked car.

FEELING DOES NOT EQUATE TO EMOTIONAL

Feeling is the decision-making process that leans toward using the filter of how the decision impacts people to complete the decision-making process. In other words, "feeler" focuses on people—*their* needs, *their* desires, and especially *their* values.

I must caution you about making assumptions. First of all, a feeler does not make decisions based on emotions any more than a thinker. As a matter of fact, if you want to see emotions, tell a thinker they have a stupid idea—that's when you will see emotion! Another misconception is that a feeler makes more illogical decisions. A thinker can just as easily make an illogical decision through the logical thought process by either using poor information or by using a preference differing from a feeler type. However, there are many characteristics that surround the feeling type.

- Feelers typically lean toward mercy before justice.

- Feelers prefer harmony and tend to avoid conflict unless it is in defense of someone who they feel has been wronged, including themselves.

- Feelers focus on relationships.

- Feelers enjoy pleasing others with enduring gestures.

- Male feelers may feel somewhat challenged in society since the characteristics are what we generally attribute to the female gender.

Since the feeler generally focuses on people and the values that drive them, they will lean more toward mercy than the thinker. It is important for the feeler to understand the "why" behind someone doing something wrong. They show mercy toward criminals more readily if there is a plausible reason for the crime that was committed. An example of this is excusing a mother who stole food for her children, because she was abandoned by an abusive husband and left with nothing.

Although the feeler will be more apt to show mercy, the feeler would prefer to avoid any conflict altogether. Harmony is the key word for those with a feeling preference. Feelers like nothing more than everyone getting along and enjoying each other's company. When conflict or a perceived conflict arises, the feeler would like to look the other way and wait for the issue to just go away.

Conflict can be a problem for some feelers, even when there is no real conflict. Many times I can see the tension and discomfort in a feeler when a couple of thinkers are chiding one another in fun. As the thinkers enjoy digging on one another in a game of one-upsmanship, the feeler is standing to the side wishing they could just get along. In fact, the feeler can logically realize that the others are enjoying the banter, but struggles with understanding why.

The need for harmony with the feeler is based on the desire for strong relationships. With the intense focus on people, the feeler enjoys strength in relationships. He will go the extra mile in making sure that relationships are continuing and will look for nuances that show the relationship is binding. A stressor in a marriage can result with the feeler constantly looking for reinforcement of the strength of the relationship while the thinker feels overwhelmed with the feeler's need for constant reinforcement. It follows the thinking statement of "I told you I loved you once, if I change my mind, I will let you know." That may be extreme, even for most thinkers, but it illustrates the thinker's frustration when a feeling spouse has a continual need for reinforcement of love.

Another hindrance to a strong relationship is guilt. Feelers have a tendency to harbor guilt more often than thinkers. Guilt can occur even if the other party doesn't feel they have been wronged. Feelers continually evaluate their performance in the relationship, whether it is consciously or unconsciously. When they feel they have done something that isn't fostering a stronger relationship, they feel guilt. This guilt can cripple some feelers who do not learn how to cope with it.

Since feelers like to test the waters of relationships, they also like to provide enduring gestures that reinforce their love for others. Small gestures of kindness or trinkets that may have no real value to others can be quite important to the feeler. The actual gesture or item isn't what is important; it is the reason behind the offering that brings importance. Flowers can be a significant gesture for a female feeler. The practicality of these expensive little items that die off quickly is minimal, but they represent the loving thoughts of the one who sent them. On the other hand, although most women love flowers, some women are not as impressed with them. Usually, it would be those women who are thinkers.

THE THINKING PREFERENCE IS NOT ABOUT BEING SMARTER

The thinking preference is more about the process than the results. "Thinkers" are not necessarily better at thinking than feelers, nor are their decisions any more logical. It's more about the logical "process" in which thinkers make the decision.

To give you an example of what I mean by an illogical thinking decision, let's look at the decision to purchase antiques for resale. I see many who have a love for antiques, decide to buy and sell them as a hobby. They spend weekend after weekend driving around to garage sales and yard sales trying to find a good buy. Occasionally, they will find what they feel are good deals, take their spoils home or to their workshop and spend time cleaning up the goods that need sprucing up. Once they have prepared enough inventory for resale, they hold their own sale. After the sale is over, they feel good about the deals they negotiated if they doubled the money they invested. They use the logical process to determine that they need to continue the hobby for financial reasons.

The logical thinking process they used was that they invested for example, $250 dollars to get a return of $500. Anyone would jump at the chance to double their money, right? Well, this logical decision becomes illogical, since there was other information that was not considered. Consider the cost of the gas they used to search for the right product to resell. This could amount to a couple of hundred dollars or more by itself. They also didn't consider the cost of materials used to clean the purchased items. Nor did they consider the amount of time used to find, purchase and resell the goods. If there was any profit at all, it would probably pay the hobbyist a few cents per hour. Pennies-per-hour is hardly the kind of money most of us would consider a worthy wage!

That is an example of how a logical process can be used to make an illogical decision. Therefore, we need to avoid the thought that thinkers are better at decision-making. They just make decisions using a different perspective.

There are several characteristics that are usually attributed to those with a thinking preference. Thinkers typically can be more objective in their decision-making than the feeler. They appear more objective because they . . .

+ Lean more toward justice than mercy.

- Focus more on ideas and things more than on relationships, sometimes to the point of pride in their objectivity.
- Can sometimes use logic at the expense of others and appear devoid of feelings.

Although the thinker shows mercy for some situations, their initial response to someone in the wrong is for justice to prevail. This doesn't necessarily refer to someone who has committed a crime. It can include those times when thinkers are faced with small challenges. I've watched thinking parents initially seek quick and decisive punishment when their child did wrong. Their initial response is justice before considering the circumstances surrounding the wrongdoing. The child did something wrong, therefore punishment is the justice that is invoked. Thinking managers I have been associated with are usually quicker to "write up" a person for punishment to deter further wrong behavior.

The objectivity in decision making, whether in showing justice or in everyday matters, can be a point of pride for the thinker. Not only can a thinker show pride for objectivity, the thinker can appear devoid of the feelings of others when making a decision.

While I was writing this chapter, my thinking wife related a story to me of a situation that is a good example of the thinker appearing devoid of feelings. We had found our home cereal challenged. The only cereal left in the house was Cheerios. With our daughters used to cereals that have a little more pizzazz, such as "Honey Nut" Cheerios, plain Cheerios was accepted begrudgingly by my youngest daughter, Samantha.

"Momma, this cereal tastes like cardboard," said Samantha.

"It's not that bad, Sam," said my wife, thinking Samantha was just being picky. In her mind the logical difference between "Honey Nut" and "plain" Cheerios is not that great.

The next morning, my wife poured herself a bowl of "plain" Cheerios only to find the taste to be somewhat "cardboardish." Then she felt bad for how she blew off Samantha's comments. (This should help the feelers to know that thinkers do have feelings of guilt, and they are actually concerned for others.) With a quick apology to Samantha, she made a point to purchase some cereal with a little more taste for the girls.

MALE FEELERS / FEMALE THINKERS

Our society's determination of what "should be" traditional male and female preferences misses the target for many male feelers and female thinkers. The feeler preferences of seeking harmony, focusing on relationships, and showing mercy and compassion, are usually attributed to the female gender. The thinker preferences of logic, justice, and a focus on things rather than relationships, are generally attributed to the male gender.

When a person finds themselves outside of the societal norm, there is pressure to conform. Therefore, the thinker female and the feeler male may work to suppress their natural tendencies in favor of behaviors that are more typical on the other side of the dichotomy. This functioning outside of their type can initiate undue stress and fatigue. To lower the stress level and improve the energy level of those who fit this category, one must work to function inside their own type preferences.

This in no way suggests that men must act as women or women as men. A man can function as a feeler by focusing on relationships and seeking harmony without having effeminate qualities. In fact, men can improve their relationships with their wives and children by focusing more on relationships while maintaining masculine qualities. On the other end of the spectrum, women can function as a thinker and be quite feminine in their actions and appearance.

Christ is the perfect example of a man who functioned in *both* the feeling preference and the thinking preference. There is no one who is qualified to judge like the Lord. Through the logical process of evaluating mankind against the laws and principles of God, He found us guilty. Yet, He was a man who showed mercy and forgiveness to those who humbly sought His forgiveness. He showed behaviors of the thinker by not avoiding confrontation when He met those who wanted to bring Him before the Roman court. He also showed feeling preferences of seeking harmony by bridging the gap between God and man. At no time do we see Jesus as a man with effeminate qualities.

STRATEGIES TO ADDRESS DIFFERENCES IN DECISION-MAKING

It would seem easy for a couple with differing decision-making preferences to work together on decisions while considering both perspectives. However, the decision-making dichotomy is more than making a decision on the obvious issues. For issues such as where to go on vacation, buying a car, or what to do on a date night, it may be somewhat simple to provide an opportunity for the thinker and the feeler in a marriage to give their perspective before making a collective decision. Problems arise from having a different mindset in how we process information. Therefore, we need strategies to understand each other's mindset. Using solid strategies, we can effectively live together as a couple with varying perspectives.

1. FEELERS NEED AFFIRMATION.

Those with a feeling preference need affirmation in their relationships, their work, and their identity. It is almost like a little test to verify that everything is good. If you have ever used a battery tester, you know that the gauge will register the strength of the current coming from the battery. Affirmation works much the same way for the feeler. It's a reading on the status of the relationship, the appreciation for what one has done for the other, and a confirmation of who they are as a wife, husband, mother, father, friend, and so on.

The thinker spouses sometimes do not recognize the need for this affirmation and must make a concerted effort to provide the affirmation needed by the feeler spouse. At first, the thinker may actually feel uncomfortable affirming more than what is natural to them. It can feel awkward and mechanical. However, if it is sincere, it isn't received as awkwardly as it feels coming out. In fact, the feeling spouse will be affirmed somewhat by the thinking spouse just making the attempt at affirming.

Affirmation can come in a variety of ways. It is the challenge of the thinking spouse to find out what tokens of appreciation work best for their spouse. It may look like a small gift at a time when it is not expected. Flowers or a small item related to a hobby they enjoy, may intrigue the wife. Tickets to a ballgame or an item related to a hobby may affirm the husband. Affirmation may also show through an act of service. The husband cleaning the dinner table for the wife or the wife taking out the trash for the husband may work. The key to affirming the feeler is to make the gestures with regularity rather than waiting to do something fantastic only occasionally.

2. THINKERS ARE NOT DEVOID OF FEELINGS.

As a child, I used to enjoy the Warner Brothers cartoon with two dogs named Spike and Chester. Spike was a large strong bulldog. Chester was a little terrier who idolized Spike. In fact, Chester would bounce around Spike telling him how strong he was and telling the audience that Spike was his hero. The little dog constantly brought up ideas of things they could do together then check for affirmation by repeating the phrase "what d'ya think?" Spike never looked impressed and rarely showed emotion. At times, he even looked irritated by the constant questioning of the friendship.

I have seen many thinking/feeling couples that remind me of the interaction of the two dogs in the cartoon. The feeling spouse consistently looks to the thinking spouse for affirmation on what seems like every word or action. This is not only draining for the thinking spouse, it is an irritant to those who have to watch it.

Affirmation is good, and it is the right thing to do on occasion. However, when one has to drag it out of the other, it loses some of its validity. Feelers who catch themselves constantly trying to drag affirmation from the thinking spouse should re-evaluate their strategy.

Thinkers do have feelings, even though they may not be vocalized as much as the feeler would like for them to be. Remember, their focus is not toward people and how they are affected. They may not be as quick to notice the other's need for affirmation, so the strategy for the feeler who is seeking affirmation should be "less is more." In other words, look for a complement or appreciation less often, and when it occurs, the affirmation will be more meaningful.

Another way to catch the notice of the thinking spouse is to work with them on their logical level. Show them the ability that feelers have to use their intellect to make solid decisions. The key is to focus your discussion on why your decision makes logical sense. Ultimately, that is what will win over the thinker and they may just show a little affirmation for your sound decision.

Let's get back to the important part of the cartoon. In the end, Spike changed places with his little buddy. He was the one who idolized the little dog, who never had to seek affirmation again. Spike willingly affirmed the friendship on a continuous basis.

3. FEELERS CAN HOLD GRUDGES

The intensity in which feelers value relationships can have an impact on the grudges they retain. When a feeler feels that they have been wronged and has bitter feelings about the person who wronged them, they avoid further conflict and harbor a grudge instead. "I don't want to talk to that person again" can be the battle cry for the feeling grudge holder.

Holding onto bitterness can be destructive and the Bible clearly cautions us about it.

> Let all bitterness and wrath and anger and clamor and slander be put away from you, along with malice. Be kind to one another, tender-hearted, forgiving each other, just as God in Christ also has forgiven you. (Ephesians 4:31–32)

Now, as a feeler, using the logic that bitterness is wrong because the Bible tells us so, is not always enough to get us past it. A strong strategy must be used by the feeler to get past the bitterness they know is wrong.

Feelers should first realize that the affects of bitterness extend beyond the one whom they begrudge. In fact, it affects the bitter feeler more than anyone else.

> The heart knows its own bitterness, and a stranger does not share its joy. (Proverbs 14:10)

The situation worsens when feelers are wronged, they can share their frustration in an attempt to lead others into siding with them. The "sharing" can lead to gossip as well. In addition, bitterness alters the mood of the one who holds the grudge, making them less desirable to be around. The affects of their bitterness not only hurt themselves, but it affects the relationships that feelers hold so dear.

To move past the grudge, a feeler should engage their preference for mercy and extend it toward those who don't deserve it. Christ was the example of the One who really deserves to hold a grudge and cut off any relationship with us for eternity. However, He extended love and mercy and suffered for us, so that we can have everlasting life with Him. Feelers should revel in the chance to suffer for Christ's sake. It is in those instances when we extend mercy that others can see Christ in us—even those who don't know Him. What an opportunity to be a witness of His love!

FAMOUS THINKERS AND FEELERS

The Bible is full of examples of those with either the thinking or feeling preference. David and Matthew write with a flair for the feeling preference, while John wrote in a manner fitting of the thinker.

When we look at the writing of the Psalms by David, we see an individual who focused on himself and others. His passion for relationships is evident in more than his relationship with God. We can also read of David's love for his friend Jonathan, who was a lifelong friend.

Matthew shows his flair for feeling by focusing on the people aspect of his faith. He opens his writing by providing evidence of Jesus fulfilling the prophecy of the Messiah. Matthew provides us with the bloodline of Jesus that shows the prophetic fulfillment through people. He continues with touching stories of the relationship of Joseph and Mary complete with the hardships in their relationship and the triumph of overcoming them to a harmonious marriage.

Other famous feelers include a couple of national politicians former Democratic Presidents Bill Clinton and Jimmy Carter.

The thinking preference is illustrated in John's writing. The focus of the book of Revelations is on symbols of faith. Candlesticks and monsters are the used to represent Christ and the evil one. Even when John refers to people, the focus is on more impersonal group identifications rather than on individuals.

Other famous thinkers include a couple of Tennessee politicians, Democrat Al Gore and Republican Lamar Alexander.

Again, a variety of heroes and villains can be found on both sides of the preference dichotomy of decision-making. Consider your own tendencies as to which side of the dichotomy you feel most comfortable. Are you the kind of person who focuses on how people are affected or are you one who considers things logically with more impartiality?

Chapter 7

THE 16 TYPES OF MYERS-BRIGGS

Myers-Briggs is a dynamic interaction of the four dichotomies of personality. In this chapter, we will look at some of the basics of a complex personality type model and put together your "type."

The four dichotomies of Myers-Briggs give us a possibility of 16 different type combinations (see table). The intricacies of the dynamics of individual letter combinations can be quite complicated. Fortunately, the purpose of this book is not to take us into a master's level discussion on Myers-Briggs dynamics. The purpose is to provide you with a starting knowledge of type preferences that will assist you in understanding yourself and others. Hopefully, you will find this information on personality type helpful enough to continue the quest for more knowledge of how type dynamics really work. The extra effort to learn more about it will be highly beneficial to you and with those you love.

PREFERENCE VERSUS BEHAVIOR

You may have read where the child's personality is formed during the first few years of life. The theory of Myers-Briggs dictates that a child is born with certain personality preferences that will prevail throughout life. On the surface, this appears to be conflicting, but in reality it is not.

The two statements are actually speaking of two separate theories on personality.

Where personality is developed in the early years, we are generally speaking of behavior. Behaviors are learned and relearned during our lifetime as we experience positive and negative reinforcements that mold our actions. When we experience a positive reinforcement for our actions, we repeat the behavior. When we experience a negative reinforcement or punishment, we change our behavior until we receive positive reinforcement. Many of the personality assessments you may have taken in the past measures behavior. Therefore, behavior-based personality assessments can change somewhat throughout your life.

On the other hand, Myers-Briggs gives us an indication as to our innate preferences. These preferences basically do not change through our lives. There are times when our behavior changes and we feel that our preference changes, when in fact they have not. Essentially, preferences are a gift from God at conception, and remain with us throughout our lives. God forms us based on His desire for us. This is evident when He spoke to the prophet Jeremiah.

> *Before I formed you in the womb, I knew you, and before you were born I consecrated you; I have appointed you a prophet to the nations.* (Jeremiah 1:5)

God had already made appointments and plans for Jeremiah before He even formed Jeremiah in the womb. It is safe to assume that He has done the same for us.

Now that I have separated preference and behavior, let me say that they are not totally unrelated. It is true that you cannot predict behavior based on preference, but preference can influence our behavior. It's the classic argument of genetics versus environment. In this case, both genetics and environment influence our actions. A person who is the more spontaneous perceiver, but grew up in a home where everyone else where judgers and preferred everything planned, will tend to have more developed planning skills. An extraverted person who was raised in an introverted home may tend to develop more introverted skills.

There is nothing wrong with learning behaviors that are opposite of what is preferred. However, there are problems that may arise when one is forced to continually behave or work outside of their preference without the chance to develop within their preference. This can be compounded when a person is raised to believe their preferences are wrong. Again, personality type is a gift from God, and should be allowed to flourish within each person, so that they may follow the will and plan of God.

At this point, you probably considered which of the four letter combinations most likely fit you. If not, I would encourage you to stop reading, review the last four chapters and see which four letter combination best describes you. The description for each dichotomy of type does not have to fit you perfectly; it only has to be the best description of the two choices. This will help you as we discuss the interactions between dichotomies.

YOUR TYPE

I recommend taking the MBTI to help determine your personality type. I would also recommend getting your type interpreted by a qualified individual or attending a MBTI class in which you discover your type as the class unfolds. This will help you in identifying your type with greater clarity. A qualified person can help you in avoid mistakes through the process. I have personally witnessed situations where individuals received information that was completely opposite of what is acceptable in MBTI practice. The result was misinterpretation of type, and improper strategies were used to try to improve particular situations. Instead, problems were made worse.

If you haven't had the chance to use a qualified person to help you, there is nothing wrong with beginning your *own* exploration of your *potential* type. Below is a chart that will help you determine your type.

In the chart, determine the best option for each dichotomy. List the letter of the option you choose in the far right column.

Extraversion: Draws energy from others, tends to think out loud, typically more social.	**E**	
Introversion: Draws energy from within, tends to think internally, may be slightly less social.	**I**	_____
Sensing: Detail and fact oriented, focused on the present, tends to be more literal.	**S**	
iNtuition: Concept or theory oriented, focused on future possibilities, tends to be more abstract.	**N**	_____
Thinking: Focuses decision making on logic, can appear less sensitive.	**T**	
Feeling: Focuses decision making on people, appears more sensitive to others.	**F**	_____
Judging: Orients to the outside world through plans, lists, and organization.	**J**	
Perceiving: Orients to the outside world through spontaneity and living for the moment.	**P**	_____

Your type is listed in the order on the table from top to bottom, beginning with the direction of energy and ending with your orientation to the outside world. Your type should look like ISTJ, ENTP, INFJ, etc.

ATTITUDES ARE MORE EVIDENT

The attitudes, or the first and last letters on your type, are usually the most evident of the four dichotomies. It stands to reason that these two dichotomies would naturally be more evident to other people. One of these dichotomies determines which direction your energy flows. Energy is either drawn from other people, or it is drained by being around others. The other dichotomy determines how you orient yourself to the world around you. You are either structured or more spontaneous.

SJ	SP
• Since SJ are usually the good soldiers, sex can be a dutiful task to perform. • Can be viewed a serious endeavor. • May not be the one to initiate creativity, but still may appreciate the creativity of their spouse. • May be somewhat structured of when and where sex should occur. Although they may not be against it in other times and places, SJs may not be usual initiator of new times and places.	• SPs are usually more reactive to real, concrete images of sex and love. Symbolism may not be quite as effective. • Typically view sex as a fun, action-oriented activity that is to be enjoyed to its fullest. • Usually appreciates variety in sex and can be a little creative, although not to the extent of intuitive creativity.
NT	**NF**
• Since NTs like to explore the logical complexities of life, sex can be somewhat of an academic endeavor. • Typically like to search out the possibilities of sexual interaction. • May not approach sex as warm and romantic as other types. • View of sex may be complex and difficult for others to understand	• Can bring a greater excitement and romance to sex than the NT counterpart. • May be more interested in symbolic images of love and sex which can peak the interest. • Appreciates the depth of the relationship that usually coincides with sex and marriage.

Small children show their attitudes at early ages. According to Elizabeth Murphy in *The Developing Child*, "The preference for attitude becomes apparent from an early age and does not appear to fluctuate."[5] Some children will give more thought to new ideas (introverted) before answering while others blurt out their first thought and may change their mind as they blurt out new and better ideas (extraverted). As they play, some children will establish how games will be played complete with rules (judgers) while others dive right in and play, then make the rules as they go (perceivers). Again, these are some generalities and are not completely indicative of a child's type. However, after careful study of your child's general behavior, you may be able to identify their preferences.

Attitudes are also generally more evident in adults. This is why there seems to be more conflict with the E/I (the external processors/ the internal processors) and the J/P dichotomies (the structured and organized/spontaneous) with married couples. More times than not, couples I advise have issues in their marriage that stem from conflicts with this portion of their types. Again by nature, the attitudes are more readily seen by others. Since they are most easily seen, they are also the areas that can cause most of the irritation for the spouse.

When conflict arises in marriage consistently for similar issues, look at conflict in one of the attitudes first. If there is conflict in the attitudes, start with strategies to ease the strain with E/I and J/P dichotomies. Using strategies that were mentioned in chapters three and four may help.

FUNCTIONS ARE LESS EVIDENT BY NATURE

Functions by nature are not always as evident as the attitudes. These functions, the data-gathering function and the decision-making function, are slightly more internal than the attitudes. Even when the person is using a function in an extraverted way, the function can still be somewhat internal. For example, someone can be "thinking out loud" which is using the thinking portion of the decision-making process in an extraverted manner. However, you are not hearing everything they are thinking about. So, some of the thinking process is still internal.

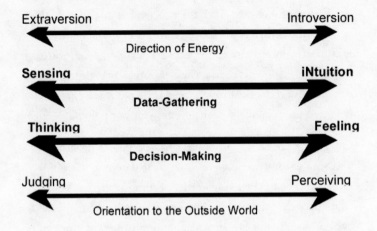

Myers-Briggs Dichotomies

Extraversion ← Direction of Energy → Introversion

Sensing ← Data-Gathering → **iNtuition**

Thinking ← Decision-Making → **Feeling**

Judging ← Orientation to the Outside World → Perceiving

How you use the functions are dependent on the attitudes. There is a dynamic interaction between the functions and the attitudes. This part of Myers-Briggs took me a couple of years to really grasp. As I stated earlier, the purpose of this book is not to delve deep into the intricacies of type dynamics. It is to provide the reader with the basic understanding of personality type to improve marital relationships.

So if functions tend to be more internal, how does an individual use functions with their spouse?

You can improve your knowledge of your spouse's functions by knowing them intimately. Listening closely to your spouse while observing their actions, will help to reveal more of how they use their functions. For example:

> While a date with your spouse, you notice that your mate is talking about the day's events and the plans for the coming days, instead of focusing on the purpose of the date and romance. You may realize that your spouse has a need to get some simple *decisions* made from all the information (or data) that they took in through the day. They have been busy with work or with children, and did not have the time to work

through their function of decision-making. Although you are ready for romance, your spouse needs to work through the internal functions. *After* the process has been finished, your spouse is then ready for romance. Your initial tendency is to push your spouse to forget the day's events and focus on the two of you alone as a couple. But, allowing them the opportunity to work through their thinking preference can heighten the enjoyment of the evening for both of you.

Or, you notice that your spouse has become a little quiet and somber one evening. You ask what is wrong with him or her, and he or she tells you that nothing is wrong. As you think back through the evening, you realize that your spouse cooked one of your favorite meals and ran an errand for you without being asked to do it. You quickly come up with a way to reaffirm your love for him or her and quit what you are doing to focus on them. You notice that they immediately perk up and the evening improves. The need for affirmation is a tendency of a feeler. If they show other feeler tendencies, you can assume that they are a feeler type.

Watching the tendencies of another person and attempting to fig-ure their personality type is called "typewatching." Although it is not perfect in figuring someone's personality type, it can often help you to narrow down a person's type and improve a relationship.

INTERACTION BETWEEN THE FOUR DICHOTOMIES

As I just mentioned, there is a dynamic element as the dichotomies interact with one another. Each particular part of preference reveals only a portion of a person, and that portion is influenced by the other parts of their personality. This is referred to as "whole type."

Whole type provides us with a clearer picture of tendencies of a per-son. It can help us to determine which function (sensing, intuition, feel-ing, or thinking) is our strongest function and which function will be our weakest. The following table will give you a summary of the function rank within each type. The top function listed under each type is the strongest function for that type while the last function listed is the weakest.

ISTJ	ISFJ	INFJ	INTJ
Sensing	**Sensing**	**iNtuition**	**iNtuition**
Thinking	Feeling	Feeling	Thinking
Feeling	Thinking	Thinking	Feeling
iNtuition	iNtuition	Sensing	Sensing
ISTP	**ISFP**	**INFP**	**INTP**
Thinking	**Feeling**	**Feeling**	**Thinking**
Sensing	Sensing	iNtuition	iNtuition
iNtuition	iNtuition	Sensing	Sensing
Feeling	Thinking	Thinking	Feeling
ESTP	**ESFP**	**ENFP**	**ENTP**
Sensing	**Sensing**	**iNtuition**	**iNtuition**
Thinking	Feeling	Feeling	Thinking
Feeling	Thinking	Thinking	Feeling
iNtuition	iNtuition	Sensing	Sensing
ESTJ	**ESFJ**	**ENFJ**	**ENTJ**
Thinking	**Feeling**	**Feeling**	**Thinking**
Sensing	Sensing	iNtuition	iNtuition
iNtuition	iNtuition	Sensing	Sensing
Feeling	Thinking	Thinking	Feeling

Although you will use all the functions to some degree, there is a definite strength in certain functions for each type.

When using personality type to improve relationships, there are a few rules of ethical use that we should consider.

+ Type can identify preferences, but it cannot predict exact behavior or skills. Never put people in a "box" and limit their ability to do anything.

+ Type should not be used as an excuse. It can explain tendencies, but it cannot be used as an excuse for poor performance in a relationship.

+ Type does not predict compatibility or love.

God doesn't put us in a box and limit our ability to accomplish a task. In fact, He considered man able to accomplish anything he puts his mind to. Consider the story of the Tower of Babel. God was upset with man because mankind in the story was trying to make his own way to heaven. God acknowledged that mankind could accomplish anything he could conceive in his mind.

> The Lord said, "Behold, they are one people, and they all have the same language. And this is what they began to do, and now nothing which they purpose to do will be impossible for them. (Genesis 11:6)

Take notice that God did not limit man's ability or personality He only confused the communication. It is communication, not personality type, that limits man. So if God did not limit us as to our personality, neither should we. Type is not a predictor of behavior, so for us to say that another person cannot do something because they have a certain type is just not accurate.

As highlighted in the second point, we should not use our type as an excuse for poor performance in a relationship. Because your preference may be for more spontaneity and less planning, that is no excuse for failing to plan a nice evening for your spouse. Because you may have a preference for using a logical process to make decisions, that is no excuse to fail to consider the impact on your spouse or other people when making a decision. There are many other situations in which we can use the excuse of our personality preferences for why we don't follow through on our responsibilities. However, we have an obligation to meet our spouse at the point of mutual satisfaction. Putting aside our preference for a short period of time to meet his or her needs is essential to maintaining a healthy marriage.

The last ethical point is that type cannot be used to predict compatibility or love. My wife and I have been married for over twenty years. During the writing of this book, I finally looked at our whole type comparison. The results were fascinating to me, because I realized we utilize our functions in complete opposite of one another. That's right, my wife and I function completely opposite of each other.

Despite our seemingly opposing personalities, we love each other deeply, and we get along quite well. That is not to say that we don't have our moments of disagreement. And, it doesn't mean we don't have some different hobbies and interests. Together we share an appreciation for lying on the beach, for playing board games with our daughters, for sitting by the fire, and for quiet dinners in a nice restaurant. On the other hand, I love sports and she does not. I have a real affinity for college basketball and am a season ticket holder for Belmont University basketball. My wife goes to the games because she wants the family to be together. She learned to appreciate the excitement of the games over the years, but sports are still not her great love. She loves to go shopping for certain things and she enjoys scrapbooking. I will go with her and make a day of shopping for things she enjoys. I support her with her scrapbooking as much as I can, but I don't enjoy those things. The point is, although we have seemingly conflicting personalities; we are very compatible and are deeply in love with one another.

We have close friends who vary in personality compatibility. Some couples have opposite preferences while others are identical or nearly identical. There is no pattern to which couples would have a strong and compatible marriage and which couples would struggle to get along.

One couple we are close to enjoys a strong marriage. According to their personality types, they are vastly different in their preferences. Yet, they have a keen sense of those differences and work hard to see that each other's needs are met. They are a joy to be around and are a support mechanism for their friends.

We also know two couples that struggle in their marriages. Both couples have had to use counselors to help them in working out challenges in their respective relationships. One couple has differing personality types between husband and wife, while the other couple has nearly identical personality types.

What makes the marriage work is not the clash or meshing of preferences, it is the behavior each person is exhibiting. This is the very reason personality type cannot be used to determine love and compatibility. It's worth mentioning again that we can learn behaviors even though we cannot change preferences. The point of this book is to help people have a better understanding of self and of their spouse and use that knowledge to adjust some of their own behavior to meet their partner's needs. So let's take a look at putting unlikely types together.

Chapter 8

PUTTING TOGETHER UNLIKELY TYPES

Dr. Jason Kastner gets to know a lot of married couples. He is a pediatrician in Gallatin, Tennessee and a good friend of mine for the last several years. As I explained to Jason that I was in the middle of writing this book, he shared his four-letter type and asked me a rhetorical question.

"How does a couple, with everything going so well while they are engaged, get to the point where they cannot go on together as a couple?" he asked.

One answer is that we rarely see the "real" person when we are dating. Oh, they may let some of their real personality show from time to time. However, for much of the time that we see our boyfriend or girlfriend, they are showing us a person that they are not. Now before some of you get offended and defensive, it is not an intentional act to deceive the one with whom we are falling in love. We can deceive each other without ever trying.

As I mentioned in chapter two, a person can interact outside of their preference for a period of time. In most cases, the dating process allows us to let our hair down and act differently for the time we are with our future spouse. Then, after the date we can crash and recover by being ourselves.

Here's how it works:

An introverted man picks up his girlfriend after a quiet day of yard work by himself. All day he thinks about what he is going to talk about that night at dinner. He practices how he can say what he wants to say and when he wants to say it. After spending much of the day alone, his internal batteries are charged, and he is ready to see the woman he loves. She notices that he is lively and outgoing from the time he picks her up to the time he gives her the kiss goodnight. She just loves his energy and outgoing tendencies; just the type of man that attracts her attention. He goes back home satisfied with his date. He crashes on the couch and reflects in solitude about the evening.

After they marry, she sees the quiet side of her new husband. He always goes off by himself, and she can never seem to get his attention anymore. She never noticed it before they married and wonders why he is acting so differently. He can't understand why she thinks he acts so differently since they married. He hasn't changed, but she seems to need more attention now than when they were dating. She never gives him space to think. It's like she chases him around, constantly needing attention.

This fictitious couple is in for trouble if they don't learn about each other's needs and work to accommodate the needs of one another in the relationship.

GOD PUTS TOGETHER UNLIKELY TYPES

The book of Genesis illustrates God creating a partner for Adam. The partner is the person who is to be a help for Adam. In creating this helper for Adam, He specifically created someone that may have had *some* similar qualities, but they were different for the most part. Eve had two eyes, one nose, two hands, and two legs like Adam. On the other hand, there were many physical differences between the two new humans. Those differences drive an attraction that God ordains and is beautifully illustrated in the Song of Solomon.

O my dove, in the clefts of the rock, in the secret place of the steep pathway, let me see your form, let me hear your voice; for your voice is sweet, and your form lovely. (Song of Solomon 2:14)

Your two breasts are like two fawns, twins of a gazelle which feed among the lilies. Until the cool of the day when the shadows flee away, I will go my way to the mountains of myrrh and to the hill of frankincense. You are all together beautiful, my darling, and there is no blemish in you. (Song of Solomon 4:5–7)

The purpose for God to create two people who were not alike was more than just for procreation. He created each one to have varied qualities so that one could shore up the weakness in the other.

Two are better than one because they have a good return for their labor. For if either of them falls, the one will lift up his companion. But woe to the one who falls when there is not another to lift him up. Furthermore, if two lie down together they keep warm, but how can one be warm alone? (Ecclesiastes 4:9–11)

Putting two people together in marriage who are of the same personality type sounds intriguing, however, it can make both parties vulnerable. When both partners have a preference for planning, the struggle is even greater when there is a need for spontaneity, or if things don't work out as planned. Struggles can also occur when both partners feed off each other's preference for feeling and there is little attention to the logical process for making a decision. These are just two of many examples of challenges for the like-typed partners. I went to a web site that was designed to determine whether a couple was compatible based on type. Although I disagree with the concept, I input my wife and myself to see how "compatible" we were. According to the web site, we are incompatible and should not marry. I'm glad that we didn't get that advice over twenty years ago.

God places unlikely types together for our own benefit. Therefore it is unwise to purposely set out to find a personality type that is the same as yourself.

CHOOSING THE RIGHT TYPE FOR MARRIAGE

Years ago, when I attended qualification classes for Myers-Briggs, I was required to sign a statement of ethics. One of the principles we agreed to was that we would not use personality type in the process of selecting job candidates for hire. Again, people can learn behaviors that are outside of their preference. So we were not to limit one another's the abilities by way of typing.

The same principle can be said for choosing a mate. Just because someone has the same type preferences as yourself, there is no guarantee that that person will live in harmony with you. Also, putting together people of varying type is no guarantee that the couple cannot live harmoniously.

If type isn't the determining factor, then how do we go about choosing a mate? Love and faith transcends personality type. We fall in love for many other reasons than someone's preferences. This is exemplified with our relationship with our children. For most families with more than one child, there is a definite difference in the personalities between the siblings. Each child is distinct in their preferences. However, most parents will love each child, even though the child may have a different personality type from themselves. Love, in this case, transcends personality type.

Since type is not the determining factor, then we have to go to the source for our mate. God knows who He desires for you to marry. Although some would dispute this, God clearly shows us that He has plans for our lives.

"For I know the plans that I have for you," declares the Lord, "plans for welfare and not for calamity to give you a future and a hope." (Jeremiah 29:11)

We can go outside of God's plan and will for our lives, but when we desire God's best for us, we should seek Him before choosing a mate. Prayer is the answer. Our prayers should ask God to send the spouse He desires for us and for discernment in knowing who that person is when we come into contact with them. With any good plan, there is a time table for events to happen, and we should consult God to know when it's the right time to marry.

LOVE THE ONE YOU'RE WITH

Stephen Stills wrote the classic song *Love the One You're With* that was released in 1971 by the band CSNY. Stills may not have been biblically sound with the lyrics, but he made a good point with the title of this song.

If you haven't already identified one of the greatest benefits of Myers-Briggs Type Indicator, it is the focus on improved communication, which is essential in a marriage. Every aspect of personality type can lead to improved communications due to greater understanding of the other person, their preferences in how they view information, and how they process it. It also focuses on how a person receives and delivers communication, as well as how they like it structured. So understanding MBTI can vastly improve the communication process.

In fact, most of the people I have taught MBTI have commented on how much better they communicate as a couple. If you remember back to the story of the Tower of Babel, the only thing that slowed down the wayward people was a lack of communication. Can you imagine a strong marriage? Good! In the story of Babel, God said we could accomplish anything we put our minds to or imagine. So if you can imagine a wonderful marriage, it can happen. Unlike the people of Babel, we must not have a barrier in communication. Our key to realizing the dream of a better marriage is to communicate well together.

Along with communication, Paul wrote that we must be in one mind and one accord. The collective mind of the couple must be working together in the same direction. Paul wasn't asking us to have identical thoughts and identical dreams; he just wanted us to work together through understanding of our fellow man. With the greater understanding of each other through personality type, we have the ability for the family first and then the whole body of Christ to reach that unity. Jesus himself prayed for this kind of unity as was written in John 17. Wouldn't it be great to be a part of the answer to Jesus' prayer?

PUTTING TO PRACTICE WHAT YOU HAVE LEARNED

Obviously, communication may be a primary aspect in a good marriage of unlikely types, but it isn't the only thing. Applying MBTI to other aspects of marriage can also strengthen it. Learning to resolve conflict in a way that brings understanding and forgiveness, and learning how to manage stress so the couple is relaxed can result in cohesiveness. Making plans and decisions together for each partner and accomplishing tasks that result in greater satisfaction is also important.

These subjects will be covered in the next several chapters as we continue to learn more about enhancing the joining of unlikely types.

Chapter 9

THE TYPE OF COMMUNICATION THAT ENRICHES

"What would you like for dinner tonight?" asks Rayanne.

"What are my choices?" responds the cautious husband, Steve. He knows better than to recommend something that isn't already in the house.

"We can have spaghetti with Italian sausage, or sirloin steaks, or an all vegetable dinner."

Steve begins to process his options. "I have been in the mood for spaghetti lately."

As she turns toward the refrigerator to begin preparing spaghetti, she is interrupted by another thought from Steve.

"However, I haven't had a good steak in a while, and it is such a nice day outside," he continues. "It would seem a waste not to grill."

"Fine, I have them marinating," she offers.

"But, the vegetables are still fresh, since you brought them home yesterday. We could grill some of the vegetables and have a veggie plate."

A confused Rayanne just looks at him and laughs.

"What's so funny?" he asks.

"I wish you would make up your mind."

He looks at her and plainly says, "That's what I'm doing."

If you are beginning to grasp the nuances of personality type, you may see the classic differences in the communication in this story. The main challenge is the introverted wife and the extraverted husband. Her preferred style of communication is to think thoroughly before she speaks. On the other hand, the husband prefers the extraverted style of speaking-to-think. He is making up his mind as he talks it out with his wife. Unfortunately she just thinks he is crazy because he didn't think things through before opening his mouth.

There are some other factors that come to play in this process that may not be as obvious. He wanted dinner options, as would most perceivers. She wanted to plan ahead for the meal as would most judgers.

With the contrasting styles of communication, how do two people become one by communicating with understanding?

COMMUNICATE TO BE RECEIVED

I mentioned previously that the strategy of using personality type should be for you to avoid changing the other person, but instead flex your own style. Communication is no different. As a director of corporate training for a large retailer, I led many classes teaching adults to communicate effectively. The premise of those classes, and any other communication class I participated in, was to communicate in a way to be received "with understanding."

The key to communication is to present so the other person can receive it. If you are asking for directions in a foreign country and you speak the native language, you probably would use the native language. Why? Because, you are desperately wanting the other person to understand you. Communicating to people of the same language should be the same way. You should make it a habit to speak to others in the way they prefer to communicate.

In the story above, the wife became a little frustrated when the husband was using his preferred style of extraversion. What could lessen her frustration would be realizing that she initiated the discussion; therefore she should be the one to flex and prepare for him to communicate in his preferred style. By preparing yourself for your spouse's communication style, you can ease the tension and enhance the communication in your marriage.

If the table was turned in this case and the husband and wife switched their preferences, it would change the communication completely. If the husband is the introvert and he had not thought about dinner, he may not be prepared to give an immediate answer. The response would more than likely be along the lines of, "I don't know, whatever you want." For the introvert to be able to give a reasonable answer, he would need time to process the idea. In this case, the strategy would be different from the first scenario.

THE OTHER FACTORS IN COMMUNICATION

As I mentioned, the other dichotomies of MBTI are also involved in this conversation. It is evident that the husband likes to have options. When asked what he would like for dinner, options were the first thing to enter his mind. This is a possible indication that he has a preference for perceiving. She was planning ahead for the meal. This could be an indication that she has a preference for judging.

Since all the dichotomies can factor into the style of communication, how does a person develop a strategy for speaking to another? Trial and error is usually effective in learning the communication preferences of your spouse. Even when you become aware of your spouse's personality preferences through education of type, there may be some things that work well and some that don't. But a working knowledge of type preferences can give you a head start on better communication. To help with the process, here is a list of typical communication preferences.

INTROVERSION

+ Introverts prefer conversations with a slower pace. Asking an introvert for an immediate response can result in a "no" for an answer.

- New ideas have a greater chance of acceptance if the introvert is allowed time for reflection on the idea.

- The response from an introvert is usually thoroughly thought through and is not easily changed without further reflection.

- Introverts depend on their internal reflection and may not seek out their spouse's thoughts when they are comfortable with their own conclusions.

- Domination in a relationship can occur as a result of a lack of conversation. The extravert cannot force conversation therefore if the introvert chooses not to communicate; the extravert is at his mercy.

- Introverts may not like to talk out issues that arise in a marriage. Since it is rare that a marriage counselor recommends a lack of communication for a strong marriage, the introvert may need to force himself to talk out issues within certain parameters.

EXTRAVERSION

- Extraverts typically prefer the faster paced conversations. The conversations can be so energized that they are characterized by interruptions most introverts would consider quite rude.

- The first thing that comes out of an extravert is not necessarily his final answer. Since extraverts think out loud, they may change their mind as they process their thoughts verbally.

- Extraverts share their thought for the moment more freely. Because it is the thought for that moment, the thought may seem a little incomplete to others.

JUDGING

- Judgers tend to be more linear in their conversation. In other words, they have a greater tendency to discuss things sequentially and with more organization.

- Since judgers prefer closure in their discussion, they tend to work the conversation toward a decision. This becomes a problem if the conversation is seeking creativity; decisiveness can be stifling.

PERCEIVING

- Perceivers like to keep their options open as long as possible, so their conversation will generally not focus on a decision. This is typical unless the perceiver feels that it is finally time to bring an idea to closure.

- Since perceivers are more spontaneous, perceiving conversation can be like shotgun spray. Topics in the same conversation can hit a number of different targets.

FEELING

- Conversation with a feeler, who is not angry with you, can be an affirming situation. Feelers tend to naturally add more affirmation for others in their conversation.

- The focus for feelers will be on people rather than things.

THINKING

- Thinker's conversations can appear more cold and calculated than feeler's. The focus tends to be more toward logical thought. Even when the discussion is about people, the topic can lean toward what people should logically do in a given situation.

- Since the conversation leans toward logic, there will more likely be less affirmation in the conversation.

SENSING

- Sensors naturally gravitate toward the details of the topic of discussion. Therefore the conversation can lead straight to details without anyone else in the conversation understanding the overall purpose of the details.

- Sensors prefer to converse about fact and reality, and become bored or disengaged when the conversation gravitates toward creativity and theory.

INTUITION

- Intuitives love to talk about the future possibilities. They may neglect the need to talk about present day situations.

- Since the focus of the intuitive is about new and exciting ideas, they may lack giving the necessary details to engage everyone else.

When I mention conversation in the previous bullet points, I am not limiting it to verbal conversation. Written conversation can work in much the same way. Sometimes tendencies can be more evident in e-mail, where those tendencies can be somewhat exaggerated.

Whatever the conversation, it is easier to communicate your message and understand the messages of others as we learn more about the preferences of ourselves and others.

Chapter 10

THE TYPE OF CONFLICT THAT
RESOLVES PROBLEMS

Conflict is a struggle. It can be more difficult when we don't understand the root cause of the marital strife. I talk to many women and men who tell me about conflict in their marriage and they don't even realize what the real cause of the issue. The conflict escalates when the couple doesn't understand how to resolve the issue.

Conflict that resolves real problems takes three steps. First, you will want to eliminate *unnecessary* conflict. Second, understand how issues affect your spouse's type. Lastly, develop a strategy for resolving conflict *prior to* an issue cropping up.

The first move we should make is to reduce the conflicts to reasonable disagreements. Our goal should not be to eliminate conflict. Conflict is actually important in strengthening a relationship. However, it should only be healthy conflict with an effective way to resolve it. Resolution is good if it is beneficial for all parties. So let's look at what makes us mad in the first place.

THE UNNECESSARY CONFLICT

What is it that makes us mad? Is it something that someone does? You would think that we get mad at others when they do something that we feel is wrong, but this isn't always the case. In fact, many times we are not upset about what someone did, we're mad because of why they did what they did. We become more concerned with their intent than the actual action. I would say that too many times, we get mad at someone for doing something that is actually good.

Does this sound crazy? It may sound crazy, but let me illustrate what I'm talking about. Here are some examples:

A wife gets upset with a husband for surprising her with a maid service to clean the house one day a week. She says, "Why did you hire a cleaning crew? Am I not doing a good enough job?" His real intent was just as he told his wife when he broke the news to her. He wanted to give her a break, since he felt she was so busy with taking care of the kids and volunteering at church. What he didn't mention was that he was hoping that she would not spend so much time at night trying to clean the house and cook dinner, so he could spend more time with her.

The *Real* Intent: Spend quality time with his wife and give her a break.

The *Actual* Behavior: Hire a cleaning service.

A husband gets upset with his wife, because she is working overtime for the third day this week. He doesn't mind the extra money from the overtime, although he doesn't really see much difference in the money she brings home. Part of it is that he feels his wife's employer takes advantage of her inability to say no. It's becoming a trend since she has had to work overtime the last few weeks. He gets crabby about the situation, but says nothing directly to her. Occasionally, he'll make a snide remark about her working too much, but they never really talk about it. What he doesn't know is that she is saving the extra money for a present for him. She plans to give him a trip to fulfill his boyhood dream of watching a baseball game at Fenway Park in Boston.

The *Real* Intent: To surprise her husband with a lifelong dream.

The *Actual* Behavior: Earning extra money for his present.

In both of these cases, the spouse is really not upset about the actions or the results. The real concern is the perceived intent of the behavior. The wife isn't upset about having help cleaning the house. In fact, she always chided with her friends that she needed to hire a service. The husband is not upset about having the extra money, and he would be thrilled with the dream trip. However, he is more concerned with his wife's perceived inability to say no.

There are hundreds of instances in our lives where we focus on the intent. Why did she say that? Does she think she is better than me? Why is he talking to that person? Is he trying to impress her? Why is he afraid to ask for help? Is it just his pride? Why did you bring that up? Are you just trying to make me mad?

WHY? WHY? WHY? WHY? WHY?

The question of "why" someone is doing what they are doing is not necessarily a bad thing. It's more a problem when we assign the intent the other person has for his actions after we ask ourselves the question why.

When we assign the intent for someone else's actions, we put ourselves in the place of God. We are not even qualified to fully understand why we do what we do. Even the Apostle Paul couldn't understand why he did things he did. In his letter to the Romans, he confessed that he kept doing what he didn't want to do and didn't do the things he wanted to do.

For what I am doing, I do not understand; for I am not practicing what I would like to do, but I am doing the very thing I hate. (Romans 7:15)

Have you ever wondered why you act as you do? You want to eat less food, but you stop by the restaurant with the buffet. You would like to eat healthier, but stop at a fast food restaurant. You would like to spend less money, but go shopping just for the fun of it. You want to exercise, but you sit on the couch and watch TV, claiming that you just don't have the time.

God is the only expert that understands the motives behind our actions. Proverbs reveals this point of God's understanding and our lack of understanding.

All the ways of a man are clean in his own sight, but the Lord weighs the motives. (Proverbs 16:2)

Since we cannot even understand the motives that drive our own actions, should we assign a purpose behind what other people do? The answer is an obvious "no." However, in many of the conflicts between a husband and wife, the perceived intent of action raises the initial disagreement.

BREAKING FROM THE CONFLICTS OF INTENT

Cal Turner, Jr. explained a situation he was in that brought him internal conflict. Cal was the CEO for the Dollar General Corporation, a multi-billion dollar retailer. One day, one of his employees came to work with a shirt that Cal thought looked really ugly. Knowing Cal had a penchant for unique clothing styles, the young man asked Cal his opinion of his new shirt.

Cal was torn. He valued truth, which would have Cal tell this young man that he thought his shirt was hideous. On the other hand, Cal also valued love for his fellow man. This value would push him to avoid hurting the young man's feelings. The conflict with these two values would see one value win out over the other. With Cal, the value of truth won out over love, and he informed the young man that his shirt was an ugly color.

The young man did not take offense to Cal's opinion. This probably weighed heavily on the decision Cal made, since he knew how the young man would react. Actually, it was a fun situation that brought out laughs for months to come.

This story is a prime example of the basis of our decision-making. Although we learned that feelers and thinkers use a different process in making a decision, both types use the process in conjunction with their individual value systems. Two of Mr. Turner's values came into play in his decision as to what to tell the young man—love for his fellow man and truth.

Each person has his own value system that contains a unique set of values arranged in a priority that is as unique as the values themselves. Like fingerprints, no two value systems are the same. With values being the basis for decisions and each person's values being unique, no one will agree with every decision made by another person. Without complete agreement, there will eventually be conflict. And, without our own understanding of why we decide to do what we do, we cannot explain away some of the decisions we make. We will make good decisions with poor intentions and poor decisions with good intentions. That being the case, we need to spend less time on considering the intentions behind an action, and spend more time deciding if the actual behavior or action is something we like or don't like.

One way to avoid focusing on another person's intentions is to recognize when we use the word "why." Why did he do that? Why did she say that? Why are they avoiding me? Why is he so quiet? Why is she spending so much money? Why won't he listen to me? When you catch yourself applying "why" to a situation, determine if it is the action that raised the question "why" that is upsetting to you. If it is not, re-evaluate to see if the "why" is really worth getting upset about.

Understanding some of the unnecessary reasons for conflict can reduce the number of conflicts as well as stress. Avoiding unnecessary conflicts is a positive step in a marriage. However, conflict will still arise from time to time. Let's look at resolving conflict in a positive way.

COMMUNICATING THE RESOLUTION

At this point of the book, you have probably figured out some reasons for conflict in your marriage. You may have also figured out why communication in conflict isn't working as well as it could for your marriage. What can't be lost in our discussion of conflict is that identical personality types can still have conflict. Conflict is not based on differing personality type; it is based on many other factors. Yet, the resolution of conflict can be more positive when we understand how each type works through conflict with communication being the key.

Most of you are well aware that marriage counselors are quite busy in resolving conflict with couples. Have you ever considered the real purpose of the counselor? The counselor rarely solves the problems. In fact, counselors are trained not to solve the problems of their clients. They are taught to assist the client or clients in working through and resolving their own issues. In the case of marriage counselors, they are trained to encourage the couple to talk out issues. I have yet to hear of a counselor recommending that a couple resolve their issues without effectively communicating.

With communication being the simple answer to complex problems, how do so many marriages falter because of it?

Much of the communication in conflict is not effective. Effective communication happens when two people convey understanding to one another. Yelling, screaming, or deathly silence rarely communicate understanding. It wasn't by accident that the previous chapter dealt with communication. Understanding communication in general is important to having a better grasp as to how it is affected in conflict.

In many conflicts, we see some of the outward manifestation of attitudes. We can see the quick and sometimes biting remarks of the extravert. We can see the struggle of the introvert to process new information and come back with a well-thought out response. We can see the judger who wants to reach closure on the discussion before the situation is ready for compromise. We can see the perceiver who takes the conflict in several different directions and adds confusion to the discussion. We can see these outward symptoms of conflict, but the core issue or issues may be more of a result of the functions instead of the attitudes. Remember, the functions are the dichotomies of Data-Gathering and Decision-Making.

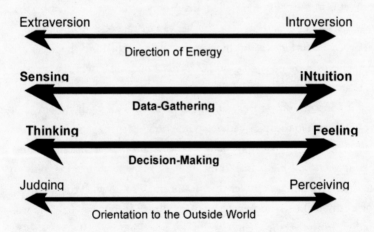

Myers-Briggs Dichotomies

Extraversion ⟷ Introversion
Direction of Energy

Sensing ⟷ iNtuition
Data-Gathering

Thinking ⟷ Feeling
Decision-Making

Judging ⟷ Perceiving
Orientation to the Outside World

We make many decisions during the day that we don't consider real decisions. These are mundane, apparently insignificant decisions. Do I turn to the right for the kitchen or do I turn left and go to the living room or do I even remember where I was going? Do I make myself a bologna sandwich or a ham sandwich? Do I wash a load of whites or do

I do a load of darker colors first? These relatively low impact decisions are similar to or exactly what causes conflict.

The choice of which load of laundry to begin with doesn't seem to have a major impact on the daily affairs of the household. However, if the husband ran out of white briefs, and the wife started a load of darker colors before he could get to the laundry room, we have a conflict. He's mad because she never considered that he wanted to pack his clothes for an early morning flight. She never seems to consider his needs before she starts tasks. She doesn't understand his problem. It makes perfect logical sense to her to wash the whites last, since there may be some bleach left over in the drum that could get on the colored clothing.

Here is an example of a feeling husband who feels his wife does her tasks without considering others. She is the logically thinking wife. She developed a plan that she habitually follows. In this example, the conflict is in the thinking/feeling dichotomy and internal function that has external ramifications. The thinker can irritate others with the logical process that focuses on things rather than people, and the feeler can irritate others by becoming overly focused on people while neglecting logic at the appropriate times.

Conflict not only arises within the decision-making dichotomy, but it can flourish in the data-gathering function of sensing and intuition as well. A sensing spouse may focus on the details of a situation and miss the big picture. One man I know will ask his wife a question, only to have her give him an answer that has nothing to do with the question. For example, he asked her if she wanted him to put the bags he was holding in the kitchen. She responded by telling him the contents in the bags, and when she planned to empty them. By this time, his arms were getting tired, and he still didn't know if she wanted him to put the bags in the kitchen. She provided much more information or detail than was needed without ever answering his question. On the other side of the dichotomy, the intuitive spouse may appear like his head is in the clouds and miss an important detail. A spouse may show his love from time to time, but miss specific dates or times that are important.

When the date is an anniversary or birthday, the situation can become an issue. When the time that is overlooked is when they agree to meet, the situation can become an issue.

Together, the data-gathering and the decision-making functions can be the source of many conflicts. Yet, there can be resolution through the use of these functions.

POSITIVE RESOLUTION

Steve Gill is a talk radio host in Nashville, Tennessee. He was also my adjunct professor for a negotiations class at Belmont University. There was a point in his class that he emphasized—both sides need to win. He did not advocate one side strong-arming the other side. He preferred negotiations to have both sides receive a fair and equitable resolution.

Resolution is positive when all parties win. A win doesn't necessarily mean that one person is right while the other is wrong. In fact, in conflict, both persons may be right or both may be wrong. A win-win resolution doesn't worry about who is right and who is wrong. The win-win resolution concentrates on how we are going to move forward toward a better relationship.

Working through a resolution can be tough. Preferences can get in the way as well as emotions. Some of you with the thinking preference may be shouting "amen" to the emotions getting in the way. However, thinkers have emotions too. You build up emotions of anger, hurt, disappointment, frustration, and more. We don't want to eliminate the emotions in conflict; we want to use the emotions to help us through the healing of the conflict.

One of the best ways in which to work through emotions is to recognize them. For years, I would teach company executives to change their approach to dealing with people's emotions at work. They would typically either not respond at all to an emotional person, or they would "develop" their people by telling them they were too emotional. I taught them to change the response from avoidance with an emotional person to acknowledging the emotion. Once the emotion is acknowledged, the emotional person has the ability to reduce the intensity of the emotion.

Acknowledging the emotions of your spouse can be somewhat tricky and a little risky, but the payoff of resolved conflict can be a blessing. One of the best ways to recognize the emotion is to ask what he or she is feeling. Get ready, because it may come more forceful than is comfortable. However, letting them tell what the emotion is, rather than discussing the episode that brought on the emotion, can be easier. Another way to bring out the emotion is to guess the emotion. You may say, "You're angry, aren't you?" Your spouse may agree with you or correct you. Either way, the emotion is identified and out in the open.

With the emotion out and expressed, the real resolution can begin. This is where the strategy using personality type can be effective. Knowing the strengths of the other and using them to reach reconciliation, leads toward long-term solutions.

Much of conflict resolution relates to communication. Here is a table of strengths and weaknesses of each dichotomy with respect to conflict resolution.

	Strength	Weakness
Extravert	Naturally more apt to express his position in conversation.	Can be overpowering in conversation. Tends to interrupt, not allowing the other person to fully express their position. May speak before fully thinking out their position.
Introvert	Will generally consider the both sides of the situation prior to speaking and will tend to avoid interrupting the other person.	May struggle with seeing the other person's position from a perspective other than their own, especially when combined with the Judging preference. May struggle with a new thought that they did not have time to process internally.
Sensor	Will generally remember details of the situation more clearly.	May spend too much time revealing every detail that is causing conflict to the point of saturation. May not see the overall problem or recurring problem because they are too engrossed with details.
Intuitive	Naturally can see trends in conflict and can work toward long-term resolution.	Can miss the little things that can cause irritation. May also get details wrong in conveying specifics to the other person.
Thinker	Can logically work toward a solution to the conflict.	Can miss opportunities to reaffirm the other person, especially when reaching a resolution. Can also miss seeing how something can affect a feeler when there is no logical explanation.
Feeler	Can affirm the relationship throughout the process of resolution.	Can lose sight of logical explanations. May also reach a point where everything is about them.

Judger	Can move the discussion from endless conversation to completion.	May try to close the discussion before a consensus has been reached. May struggle to see the other person's position, especially when combined with introversion.
Perceiver	Can make sure all points have been covered before closure. Is usually good at seeing the perspective of both sides.	Can avoid closure of the topic and raise too many other unrelated or semi-related topics.

To use this table effectively, you must build a strategy using the information prior to the conflict. Realistically, when you are in the middle of an argument, the chances of you rationally considering the table information are slim. It works best when the couple can sit down and work out a process to resolve conflict when there is no conflict at that moment.

A good start toward building an effective strategy for conflict resolution comes from identifying the strengths of the spouse. If you have an idea of the personality type of your spouse, identify their strengths using the previous table. You will use these strengths to resolve the issue. Next, identify your type and the weaknesses that are associated with your type. It may not feel good to realize what area is not your forte, but coming to grips with your weaknesses will go a long way in harmony with your spouse.

Your spouse's strengths and your own weaknesses are the building blocks of a process that can turn a conflicting situation into model of harmony.

THE PROCESS

When I taught communication courses in business, I found the process itself to be quite simple. It was the execution that made communication tough. In most cases, I could give a written test on communication basics after an hour or two of class, and have most, if not all, adult students pass with flying colors. The problem was that they wouldn't be any better at actually communicating than when they came into the class. Most of the really effective classes on communication that I experienced lasted 3–5 days. How come? It takes practice to change the behavior necessary to effectively communicate.

The focus on resolution leans heavily on communication, so the process for conflict resolution will seem quite simple—and it is. However, making it happen as it is planned out on paper will take practice and forgiveness.

The process has basically three parts, as it is with most basic communication. The first part is the opening which I call "Setting the Stage." Setting the stage is short compared to the next part of the process, but it is crucial in the resolution process. The second part is what I call the "Dialogue." This is where most of the time will be spent. The last part of the process is the closure, which I call the "Closing Curtain."

SETTING THE STAGE

The opening of a play, movie, or novel, sets the tone for the story. Comedies get you laughing quickly, mysteries get you guessing right away, and love stories have you falling for the heroine before you really know her. Regardless of the form of the story, it is the responsibility of the author to set the appropriate tone for the rest of the play, movie, or book.

Successful resolution must also have its stage set by the person initiating the process. Although most people with a feeling preference like to avoid conflict, they have to remember that real harmony comes when problems are addressed and the stage set properly. The tone of the conversation to follow is strongly influenced by how the stage is set. If a man busts into a room and abruptly shouts at his wife, the stage is set for a melee. If the wife folds her arms and turns her back on her husband, there may be begging and pleading for calm, but not a lot of effective conversation. However, if a husband comes to his wife and greets her with a hug, then gently tells her that he is troubled and asks for her help, she may be more open for discussion.

The stage is set for conversation when the topic of discussion is clearly identified and the climate is set appropriately for open discussion. Again, it sounds simple, but it can be more difficult in execution. A vice-president of human resources for a major corporation once had the dubious task of firing an employee. Who better to know how this is done than a human resources executive, right? Not so. Two hours after the VP fired the employee, another employee had to let the VP know that the employee was still working. The tone of the conversation was so warm and fuzzy and the topic of discussion so unclear, the employee did not realize that he was fired. As a marriage partner, you will not have the task of firing your spouse, but this illustrates that a clear topic of discussion and an appropriate climate is important to accomplish a satisfactory resolution.

Setting the climate in a marital conflict can be tricky as with any other conflict. You are bringing up a subject that will not make him or her happy, yet you want to motivate them to discuss and resolve the issues. An appropriate climate for discussion is set by reinforcing a love for your mate, while letting him know that the subject is serious and in need of resolution. Reaffirming the love is generally a strength of the feeling preference.

You must also choose an appropriate time and location for the discussion. A quiet place, without distractions, is usually most appropriate. These days, it seems difficult to find a place where there are no interruptions, but it can happen. Turn off the cell phone and TV. Make sure the children are occupied for the moment. If possible, let the children know that mom and dad need a few minutes of private time. You find time to have sex in private; it is also possible to have a discussion in private. It's also important to find a time when your spouse is not busy. If the time needs to be scheduled, then by all means schedule the time. Judgers may appreciate having the time scheduled, or at least not interrupting their planned events. Discussions while doing time sensitive tasks, like cooking dinner, usually won't work.

The last general task in setting the stage is to identify the subject to discuss. Like our VP who had to terminate the same employee twice, not establishing a clear and specific topic to discuss may result in having to resolve the conflict a second time. Even if it feels uncomfortable to be specific about what is troubling you, it is important to be clear and precise about the topic. Having a specific topic will help in keeping the conversation from drifting to everything else that isn't perfect in the marriage. The key is to work on resolving one problem at a time.

THE DIALOGUE

The dialogue is the second stage of the resolution process. In this, the largest part of the process, the two-way conversation brings understanding to the situation and works toward a compromise. The goal here is not to win the argument; the goal is to bring a win-win situation to the marriage. Therefore you must monitor your own input to the conversation to insure that it either brings understanding of the situation or it works toward a solution.

There are three things to keep in mind when having a conversation with your spouse:

- Do not interrupt your spouse while he/she is speaking.
- Do not get defensive.
- Find points of agreement.

In a confrontational conversation, there will be things said that will not make you feel good. Controlling the urge to retaliate is challenging, but possible. Rely on the strengths of your personality type to get you through those times. Also, remember to use the strength of your spouse's type to help you with those areas that are a struggle for you. For example, extraverts tend to interrupt when a thought hits their mind. If you are an extravert, prepare your spouse in advance to point it out for you when you interrupt. When he or she points it out, you have the responsibility to accept it and move on.

To help you further utilize the strengths and weaknesses of each personality type in conversation, revisit chapter nine. That chapter will help you through the maze of conversational strengths and weaknesses. If you find yourself struggling during the conversation, ask the other person for a time out until you are able to continue with a rational discussion.

Regardless of personality type, most confrontational conversations tend to make both sides a little defensive. One of the best ways to minimize the defensiveness is to focus your attention on finding points of agreement, rather than points of disagreement. Whether it is politics, religion, or marriage, there are usually many points that both sides can agree upon. In politics, both republicans and democrats want better schools, health care, and jobs. The difference in the two is how to get our communities to have those things. In Christian denominations, there will be agreement that Christ is the Savior. Differences arise in how we worship, pray, etc. Finding the points of agreement and identifying those will help to move the dialogue in a positive manner. In marriages, both spouses desire happiness, contentment, love, and financial security, but there may be differing opinions on how to obtain them.

How do you point out the points of agreement? It isn't as hard as it might sound.

I recently experienced a conflict of ideas with a person who was a director for a state education department. It went something like this:

"We continue to rank as one of the worst states with respect to our children's test scores," said the director. "Our children should be our priority. We need more money to bring the tests scores up. Please support the current administration in their continuing effort that has already brought an additional $50 million in funding over the last five years."

"I agree that our children should be our priority," I commented. "However, you mentioned that the state has added $50 million over the last five years and the state's ranking hasn't improved. I don't see where more funding will help the test scores."

Although there was a conflict of ideas, the two of us could agree that children should be a priority. Finding those points of agreement can reduce the emotional outbursts and lead to meaningful conversation. Conversation with some agreement mixed in, shows both sides that it is not a personal attack; it is a different view. In other words, you can catch more with honey than with vinegar.

CLOSING CURTAIN

You have probably seen a movie that you thought was great, only to be disappointed with the ending. The movie may have killed off the character you liked, or it may have left too many things unanswered. Closing the curtain on dialogue intended to resolve conflict can sometimes be disappointing. Finding the right way to end conflict can leave a lasting positive feeling, where everyone wins rather than someone walking away feeling defeated.

Judgers like to have clean closure on things. When it comes to conflict, it is no different. However, that doesn't necessarily mean the judger knows when and how to close the conflict. Their desire to close the subject and move on may cause those with a judging preference to close the discussion too quickly. However, the perceiver may have the tendency to drag the conversation too long. Although there is no formula as to correct length of dialogue, practice on the process will have you getting better as to when it is time to close the curtain.

The closing should come after certain things are accomplished.

1. The issue must have been clearly defined for both sides.

2. There should be a plan as to how both sides will move forward to avoid further conflict with the issue.

3. Lastly, and probably most importantly, each person needs to reaffirm the love they have for one another.

Typically, those with a feeling preference are good at reaffirming love. However, there are times when the feeler can hold grudges or focus attention inwardly and miss the opportunity to use their strength. Regardless of your type, you must make a conscience effort to affirm the marriage.

Resolving conflict sounds simple, but putting it into effect can be more of a challenge. With some planning and rules to resolve conflict, the Christian couple can make conflict resolution a minor event with major impact.

Chapter 11

THE TYPE OF RELAXATION THAT REDUCES STRESS

"Kate" is an energetic extravert. She loves the excitement of being busy and talking to people. She has the ability to hold a conversation at a speed that would keep a court stenographer challenged, while not requiring anyone else to add to the conversation.

Her husband, "Roger," is a slower talking introverted businessman who loves to see an old friend walk through the door. He's just "one of the guys" when he is in his element. He is surrounded by familiar faces all day long at work.

When the work day is done, Roger has a short commute of about five minutes to his home. As he pulls in the driveway, he enjoys the quiet surroundings of a country home that has only pasture land as a neighbor. The thought of some quiet time to process his work day and recharge his batteries sounds great to Roger.

He is met at the door by his wife and kids who are all talking at once, with the excitement of seeing dad and telling him about their day. He smiles and enjoys the welcome with the exchange of kisses and hugs. He's now ready to clean up and wind down from the day's work. But, as he moves toward the master bathroom to clean up and change clothes, his lovely wife follows him, talking at the speed of sound. The kids have run off, laughing and screaming while they play.

Roger's eyes do not meet with Kate's while she continues to tell him about all the events of her day. He appears to be quietly listening, but the lack of eye contact isn't noticed by her as she rattles on. He heads to the living room and turns on the TV. Kate continues her recap from the kitchen, as he turns the TV up a little louder. Occasionally he mutters an "um hmm" just to let her know that he can still hear her.

The volume of the TV, along with the recap of his wife's day, is finally too much for Roger to handle. He can't seem to process the events from his own day. Although he doesn't understand why he has the urge to get up and "do something" when all he wants is to relax, he heads out the door to fix the fence that really isn't in bad shape. In the meantime, Kate wonders why her husband always feels the need to tinker in the yard when everything already looks great outside.

The problem for both Roger and Kate is that they are functioning outside of their preferences. In other words, they are spending a considerable amount of time doing those things that are not natural for their personality type. When a person functions outside of his preference for a considerable amount of time, without an opportunity to recuperate, there is an increase in the amount of stress and fatigue.

FUNCTIONING OUTSIDE OF PREFERENCE

In our previous situation, Kate is a stay-at-home mom. She is extraverted and quite expressive. She is invigorated by the interaction with other adults. However, staying at home with the children limits the amount of adult interaction she has during the day. So subconsciously she finds things to do and errands to run outside of the home to increase her opportunities for adult interaction. When she is stuck at home, she seeks out conversations with friends and family on the phone. She can't stay on the phone all day long, so she still has plenty of time where she has is no adult interaction. To compensate she must make it up when her husband gets home. The need for interaction is as strong as a healthy sex drive.

Roger, on the other hand, is introverted. Even though he is congenial with the people at work, he loves his time alone when he can internally process. After long periods of time in dealing with the public, he craves time alone to think and relax. Since he has a very short commute, he is looking for down-time at home. Yet, when he is home, he is inundated with attention that can be overwhelming for the introvert.

There are many situations where the husband and wife do not understand the needs of one another. They are missing opportunities to accommodate one another and reduce each other's stress levels. This doesn't occur with just introversion and extraversion. All four dichotomies can be affected by functioning outside of preferences. For example, someone who is a perceiver can be fatigued by functioning in a very rigid, planned, and/or routine environment. A person who prefers judging can be stressed in an environment that is extremely spontaneous. An intuitive person who must deal with specific details all day will seek a release. The opposite of the intuitive is the sensor, who seeks relief from functioning in an environment of constant creativity and blue-sky thinking. I've even know some with a feeling preference that stress in an environment with people throwing verbal jabs at one another. They want everyone to affirm one another, not tear them down—even if it is all in jest. Regardless of the preference, we live and work in environments that lie outside of our natural preference. Learning how to cope with these situations will help us to lead a more relaxed and less fatiguing life.

COPING WITH THE UNNATURAL

There is no way that we can avoid functioning on some level in a situation or environment that is not our preference. With four factors of our personality type, there is often at least one dichotomy that is dealing with a situation that is not our preference.

When I worked in the corporate world, I would find myself in situations that were both compatible *and* contrary for my personality type at the same time. It sounds impossible, so let me give you an example of what I mean. Since I was in the corporate training field, I would end up in meetings "to improve performance." Many of these meetings were brainstorm sessions where all participants were expected to give input. Meeting with a group of fellow employees would please my extraversion preference. The open discussion would satisfy my perceiving preference. However, the blue sky, forward thinking discussion runs contrary to my preference of sensing, since it is more of an intuitive function. After a couple of hours of this type of meeting, I would begin to tire. There came a point where I would get stressed and just want to make a decision and move forward, even though that wasn't the purpose of the meeting. At the end of the day, all I wanted was to relax and talk about something more concrete.

The task for us is not to avoid the stress related environments all together. The task is to learn how to cope when we find ourselves becoming stressed or fatigued due to prolonged time in a situation that is not our preference.

In defining a relaxation strategy to overcome stress, we have to first identify those situations that are outside of our natural preferences. With your personality type identified, you can review what situations are typically not your preferred environments. For example, if you have a thinking preference, an environment where there is a lot of affirming, but very little logical discussion can be tiring. Or, you may be a perceiver who finds yourself in a planned and structured environment all day.

Once the stressful or fatiguing situation is identified, you can look at how to break away to your natural preference for relaxation. It may not always be easy, but with a little creativity, you can find ways to sneak in a little regeneration.

A former associate of mine, who was introverted, worked in a situation where she was with people continuously throughout the day. She rarely took lunch to get a break from her work. By the mid-afternoon, she looked like she hadn't slept in three days and lacked in the area of patience. If she was *that* stressed by mid-afternoon, you can imagine what she would be like in the evening. Her problem was that she was in an extraverted environment with introverted preferences. My suggestion to her was to take a lunch break where she could get away either by herself or with a close friend. I even suggested that if she found herself having trouble getting away, she find someplace where she could be alone for a few minutes—even if it was in the restroom. When she took the time to refresh and relax herself in solitude, she was more congenial and more rested in the afternoon.

Each person in the marriage must evaluate the stressors they encounter during the day and find some form of relief and relaxation. However, relaxation varies from person to person and from type to type. What is relaxation for one person can feel like punishment for the next. Typically in a marriage, there are variations in what is relaxing from one spouse to the next. Not only should you look for relaxation from stress for yourself, you should develop a plan for helping your spouse find relief.

GIVING YOUR SPOUSE REST

Since we are homeschool parents, my wife assumes much of the responsibility of teaching the kids during the day. So her daily schedule begins with fixing breakfast for the kids, followed by a morning of teaching. She fixes lunch for them at mid-day, followed by *more* teaching. At the end of the day, I come home to spend the evening with the family. Where in this schedule does my wife have an opportunity for introversion? Sometimes she will make time while she sets up activities for the kids, but this time is slim. So it then becomes my responsibility to help her find those precious moments to recharge her batteries. Some evenings, I run her a bath in the Jacuzzi tub and occupy the kids while she takes time to introvert.

That works for my wife, but it isn't the recipe for everyone's relaxation. If an extravert has been working alone all day, the last thing he or she may want is a long bath alone. Knowing what preferences your spouse has will take you a long way in providing him or her with moments of relaxation. But be prepared, relaxation and recovery from stress may take on unusual characteristics. Running several miles after a day of work may not sound like recovery from stress to you. Milling around a crowded shopping center may be the last thing you want to do when you're stressed. But, for some people these activities are where they find their relief.

Helping one another find and experience those activities that reduce stress will pay huge dividends. A relaxed and happy spouse is a recipe for finding peace and happiness for you along with a happy marriage.

Chapter 12

THE TYPE OF PLANNING THAT REACHES FRUITION

"What do you want to do today?" asked Jack. He was ready to enjoy the weekend with his beautiful wife. It was a gorgeous Saturday, with the sun shining and warm breeze easing through the neighborhood.

"There's nothing I can think of to do," Jane said.

"Well, we can take a drive to the state park and have a picnic at the base of the waterfalls," he said. He just knew she would go for that idea. She loved the state park, which was a little more than an hour drive away.

"No," she replied.

Stunned at the decline, he scrambled for another idea. "How about driving down and spending the day at the theme park?"

"No, I don't feel like doing that today."

"Well, we can go to the mall, or we can go to the theater to see that movie you wanted to see," he said, beginning to see the futility in his attempts to please her. "Or, we can go to the zoo or museum. You said you wanted to see those places."

"No"

"Well, what *do* you want to do?"

"There is nothing *to* do." she said.

Now his frustration was clearly beginning to rise. "What do you mean there is nothing to do? I keep making suggestions, so there *are* things to do, you're just being difficult."

Jane didn't even reply. She got up and stomped out of the room.

In the grand scheme of things, planning, or the lack of planning, will not necessarily make or break a marriage. Yet, so many couples struggle with simple situations just like this example. Frustration builds as one person seeks to enjoy the moment while the other wants to see some plan and organization to the day. In the case of Jane, she felt there was nothing to do because they had not planned the day in advance. The thought of doing something spur of the moment was not appealing to her. These struggles over little daily plans can be as frustrating as struggles over larger, more important plans such as the financial future of the household.

Keep in mind, it is not better to *always* plan or *always* be spontaneous. In many situations, it's okay to be either way. The frustration comes when the one who prefers judging has a perceiving spouse who seems like they never plan or organize any part of his life. Frustration can also happen the other way when the perceiver feels stifled from the over-planning or extreme organization of the judging spouse.

Challenges also arise when one feels like his way is right and the other person needs to learn how to be more like him. Keep in mind, your preference is just that—*your* preference. It may not be your spouse's preference. So, there must be a neutral ground that the couple can maintain if there are differences. If both parties in a couple have the same preference, there are a whole set of other problems. Planning to the second power can be as devastating as spontaneity squared.

SOMETIMES A PLAN WORKS

There are times when the day is ruined by either planning or being spontaneous. The day can seem exciting for the perceiver who jumps up one morning and decides to go camping. But when all the campsites are already taken when he arrives, the day is ruined. Conversely, the day can seem great for the judger when outdoor activity is planned and organized only to see it dashed when a surprise rainstorm arrives. The point is there are times when spontaneity works really well and there are times when planning works best.

There are also those times when either spontaneity or planning would work equally well depending on the preference of the individual. It's important for us to realize that since many situations will work well either way, we need to be flexible enough so that each person in a marriage can exercise his preference at one time or another.

As previously mentioned, many judgers would like to "fix" their spouse and turn them into planners and organizers. They often point to a moment where perceivers do something with little to no planning and it doesn't work out as the perceivers had thought. "See, that's what happens when you fail to plan," is the mantra of the judgers at this point. Judgers are only looking at it from their perspective. Usually, when perceivers attempt something with little to no planning and it doesn't work, they typically have the mindset to move on or adjust to fit the situation without stress. In fact, a change can make things more exciting for perceivers who do not have an issue with functioning in this manner. Yet, it can be devastating to the judger spouses.

Regardless of whether you prefer judging or perceiving, there will be some planning and organizing required in a marriage. The goal is to work out plans that give comfort to the judger without stifling the perceiver.

Situations are numerous that require planning or would be improved if a couple has planned ahead. For example, financial stability requires strong long-range planning. Failing to plan for future financial needs can result in escalating debt that brings stress into a marriage. Determining a career change can be successful when a couple has a good plan for the changes that will take place in the household. Failing to plan career changes can leave a household with little security and cause them difficult transition to the new lifestyle. Although children are a blessing from God, planning for the arrival of the blessing can make that life transition smoother. It's the responsibility of the couple to determine the level of planning for these major events.

Planning and organizing, the natural functions for the judger, can be both an asset and a liability for the couple. Since it is a strength, the judger should be used as a resource to organize the planning. But, caution should be used here; the judger may have a tendency to *over* organize or *over* plan in the marriage. Over-planning can get to the point that it becomes an irritant to the spouse and close friends and family.

PERCEIVERS REALLY DO PLAN

Although this may be hard to believe for most judgers, perceivers really do plan. However, the plans of a perceiver do not look like the plans of a judger, in most cases. Perceiver plans are made with two significant traits. First, a perceiver's plans are quite loose. Secondly, a perceiver usually prefers to plan tentatively with a smattering of options laced throughout the plan.

In chapter four, I mentioned that plans perceivers make are more loosely structured, loosely developed and contain options that allow the perceiver to choose a course of action depending on the circumstance. Typically, when a judger sees these loosely developed plans, they don't view them as real plans. However, the perceiver is sold on the plan unless the situation changes and then the perceiver will move in the new direction or develop a new flexible plan.

These more flexible plans are really not that bad for most situations. As a matter of fact, they can be beneficial in instances where there are unplanned and uncontrollable circumstances that force the altering of the plan. However, the judger may not even recognize that the perceiver plan is even a plan. It looks too loosely organized for them to recognize it as a plan. What the perceiver needs to realize is that a change of plans can be somewhat unnerving to the judger spouse, thereby increasing the stress level in the marriage. Perceivers would do well to include the judger in redeveloping a plan for the new situation. This will give the judger a greater feeling of control in a situation that may seem a little out of control.

Household planning should be biblical, as every other part of the marriage. Proverbs lays out a simple structure for planning in chapter 16.

> *Commit your works to the Lord and your plans will be established.* (Proverbs 16:3)

According to this Psalm, the process is to commit our works to the Lord and our plans will succeed. However, there is more to this than just making plans and saying they belong to the Lord. There is the "C word" that many in our society have aversion to—commitment. Commitment of plans is more than just saying that you are making plans that honor God, or that they are your attempt to please God. Commitment of plans to God means that God is involved in the planning right from the start, making Him the focus until completion of the plan. You may be thinking that I am talking only about large, grandiose plans, but I'm also talking about the seemingly mundane plans of what to do during the day.

There are reasons that God requests us to rise early and meditate on His word. The purpose is to focus our attention on the One that can guide us through the daily tasks that await us. He already knows what the day will bring, and He already knows the plans He has for you. Consulting with the Lord first thing will bring a greater perspective on what our day should include.

Initiating plans with the Lord requires at least two things: guidance in prayer and guidance through His word.

PLANNING WITH THE BIBLE

Plans should never be contrary to God's word. Because of this, knowledge of His word is essential. Studying the Bible each day can help us to develop large and small plans throughout that day. As we read the Word, the Holy Spirit reveals to us more of the mind of God and what His purpose is for us. There are so many answers in the Bible for our daily plans, that we can read it everyday for the rest of our lives and still receive new application in those last days.

Here is how reading the Bible can help you in daily plans. Say you are a stay-at-home mother, and you have sent the children to school and are at the kitchen table reading the Bible. You have planned to do your shopping while the kids are at school. You also plan to meet with a couple of friends for lunch while you are out. Then you will pick up the kids from school, help them with homework, and prepare supper. As soon as your husband comes home, the family will eat and rush off to soccer games. You know that at the end of the day, you will be exhausted. Your house needs to be cleaned, and the laundry is getting behind. While you are reading the Bible, you come across a scripture that discusses the busyness of the day and the characteristics of the prudent woman. You decide that since plans for shopping were only because you enjoyed it, you eliminate that task. You decide that you can put off having lunch with your friends, since you met them for lunch a couple of times last week. You can also re-evaluate the soccer games that occur several nights a week. At the end of the day, you find yourself not nearly as tired and frustrated. The Bible study helped you to see what should have priority, according to the Lord.

PRAYERFUL PLANNING

Prayer is another way to commit your work and plans to the Lord. Jesus is given the name of Wonderful Counselor in the book of Isaiah. We have access to the One who can give us great counsel on how our plans should be made. He is One who knows the future and knows us. He can let us know when our plans are good, or when they will not be a benefit for us. By prayer, we can seek what the Lord desires for us.

For many, prayer seems like a one-way street—an extraverted activity with a God who just sits and listens. This couldn't be farther from the truth. We are to bring our petitions to the Lord in prayer, but we are also to listen to Him speak to us. In the book of John, Christ refers to us as sheep that He cares for in the same manner a shepherd cares for his sheep. Notice the reference that we, as His people, will know His voice.

> *I have other sheep, which are not of this fold; I must bring them also, and they will hear My voice; and they will become one flock with one shepherd.* (John 10:16)
>
> *My sheep hear My voice, and I know them, and they follow Me.* (John 10:27)

Christ has an expectation for us to listen to Him in our prayerful planning. Just how does one listen to the Lord in prayer? The person praying can do it in a number of ways. He gives us peace when we share our potential plans with Him and He approves. He also confirms plans through other people.

A personal example of listening to God in prayerful planning was the story of how I found a publisher for this book. As I began to research potential publishers, I found several that I thought this book would fit into their niche. Tate Publishing came up near the top of the list as I rated different aspects of the publishers. However, I had questions about their ability in certain areas. It was a case of being too good to be true. I continued praying that God would lead me to the right publisher. During my prayers, I continued to get a peace about Tate, despite my concerns.

A friend of mine, who is in the book industry offered to read the first few chapters to offer his advice. He suggested a couple of publishers, and Tate Publishing was on the list. I asked him for his opinion of Tate, and it was favorable.

It was not long after I sent out submissions that I got a contract offer from Tate. God had let me know from the beginning when I was planning the writing of the book that Tate would be the publisher. He gave me peace as I prayed, and He sent wise counsel my way to confirm what I thought the Lord was telling me.

In the case of the planning for this book, I committed the work to the Lord and He established the plan.

There is a necessity for including a third party in godly marital planning—it is your spouse. God intended for the married couple to work together as one. So, planning for the married person, in most cases, should include God *and* the spouse.

God has put this important person in your life for balance and wise counsel. That doesn't mean that every piece of advice from your mate is going to be great, it just means that there is counsel available to help you to fully think through a plan. In the book of Ecclesiastes, there is a reference of a three strand cord being strong and hard to break. Marital plans made with God and your spouse are strong plans that can accomplish great things.

Including your spouse in planning can bring up interesting issues with regard to personality type. We have already covered some of the biggest challenges in type with regard to spontaneous activity or loose planning verses very organized and strict planning. However, there are more issues related to type.

The functions of Data-Gathering and Decision-Making can also affect a couple's planning. The amount of detail addressed in plans or the overall purpose of the plan is affected by the Data-Gathering function. Decision-making will address the logical aspect of the plan and who will be affected by the plan.

In general, keep in mind these tendencies by function:

+ Sensors may have a tendency to include too much detail and complication to make a plan workable and may not spend enough time considering the overall purpose of the plan.

+ Intuitives may have a tendency to concentrate too much on the overall purpose of the plan and not include enough detail to work through problems that may arise.

+ Thinkers can focus so much on what is logical in the planning process, that they may forget to include how the plan will affect the people involved—especially in the household.

♦ Feelers can focus so much on how the plans will affect people that they will ignore the logical aspect of planning.

It is wise to recognize the tendencies of your type and the type of your spouse when planning. Too much of a personality type strength can hurt your plans because the plans may have not addressed everything it needs to address. Too little attention to areas of weakness and your plans could suffer too.

OUTLINE FOR MARITAL PLANNING

There is a simple outline to make your planning successful, whether the plans are short-term plans, such as activities for the weekend, or long-range plans, such as retirement.

1. Determine the overall objective of the plan. Before adding any detail to the plan, there should be an agreement as to the objectives. In the short-term case, determining the activities for the weekend may hinge on whether the need is for stress reduction, family bonding, etc. Long-term plans may be a little more complicated. Outcomes for retirement planning may have several aspects, but they should all be outlined so all involved understand them. The objective should be determined with you, your spouse, and the Lord all in agreement.

2. Determine all of the players. In other words, who will be affected by the plans and who will be needed to complete the plans. Who will be needed to complete the plans may be somewhat tricky, but identifying those people will help you determine how to proceed. For example, when planning for children, you may want to include consulting with a doctor and a financial advisor. It may sound a little cold to include a doctor and financial advisor for planning for children, but keep in mind that the *logical* impact of those cute little bundles of joy cannot be ignored.

3. Work out the details of the plan. This is the time to gather advice from the players in the plan and any other experts that might be of some help. The plans should also include a time-line. If a timeline is not put into place, the plan may never get started, or may never end.

4. Implement the plan. During this phase, not only should tasks be completed, but there should be a review of the timeline to verify that tasks are happening according to plan.

5. The completion of the plan should have a quick review to see how well you did. If the plan didn't work as planned, then look to find what things went wrong so they can be corrected for future plans.

Successful marriages have successful planning involving both partners who use their gifts to complete plans as they are developed. Continuing to plan as a couple with God is essential and the rewards can be life changing.

Chapter 13

THE TYPE OF TASKS THAT GET COMPLETED SUCCESSFULLY

Do you get frustrated when your spouse never seems to get a task completed?

Or, do you get frustrated when your spouse starts a task and won't stop until it's completed—even if it takes all night and he or she ignores everyone and everything else?

Or, is it that your spouse never seems to do a job the right way?

Does your spouse lack a method for doing what they do?

Does your spouse always put things off until you finally nag them into finishing the job?

Are jobs around the house started, but never seem to get done?

Tasks, honey-do lists, or household jobs. You may call them a number of things, but one thing is certain; they are important in a marriage. It's not often that you hear of marriages dissolving because a couple argues over tasking. Yet, it is a source for many irritations in a marriage. Many of the irritations stem from one of the questions above.

Personality type plays a huge role in how tasks get started and how they get completed. Most of the input on the style of working tasks is the attitude of Orientation to the Outside World. The world of the judger and the perceiver is oriented by the structure and organization.

The perceiver enjoys the spontaneity of life while the judger prefers the well-planned and organized activity.

TIME MANAGEMENT IN TASKING

Many of you reading this have spent some moments in a time management class. These classes are usually written by judgers who have much of their day planned and organized. What they have learned over the years is put into a system and taught in a class. This information can be invaluable in helping us to make our days more effective. Yet, there is no time in human history when society, which is so well-versed in time management applications, has had so little time on their hands. There has never been a time like the present, when the word "busy" has been used as an adjective to describe the woman, the housewife, the career individual, the executive, and so on, and so on.

What makes this topic so difficult that we as a society do not have enough time to have a sit down dinner at home, or even enough time to rest.

One of the reasons is the complexity and inflexibility of most time management systems. There are so many ways of managing our time that it seems as if everyone should be able to find one way that can work for them. However, most time management philosophies are developed to be worked one way. The challenge is that one size does not fit all.

I received a Franklin Planner from the corporation I worked for several years ago. It was one of the premier time management tools available for the busy businessperson. To learn how to use it, I took seminars to learn how to *effectively* use it. Although there were some techniques I learned in the class that were helpful, I found the system too complex and cumbersome for my personality. A few of my peers loved the way the system worked and used it faithfully. Other peers found it not quite as useful.

Michael Hyatt, the President and CEO for Thomas Nelson Publishers, also found the Franklin system to fall short for him. In 2004, Mr. Hyatt wrote a blog that suggested the Franklin Planner system to take on the David Allen system of time management. However, he wasn't completely satisfied with that system either. He needed something that was workable for him, since his tremendous responsibilities require him to make the best use of his time. Hyatt writes that he used the Allen system and added his own modifications to make it work for him.

The point of all this is that regardless of the number of techniques and systems available for managing our time, we still struggle with not enough time at the end of the day for important things. Married couples lack the time and energy for intimate conversations, romantic dates, or even to have a few moments of sexual intimacy.

The solution is to learn about your personality, realize your challenges with managing your time, and develop your own systems to manage time that will work for you.

UNIQUENESS OF TIME MANAGEMENT BY TYPE

A whole book could be written on time management by type. Personality type can affect so much of the time management skills and needs of the individual that it couldn't be dealt with adequately in an individual chapter or portion of a chapter. I even hesitate to include it, but I feel that a little information may help you to search out the best method of managing your time.

The managing of time is significantly impacted by the last dichotomy of personality type which is the Orientation to the Outside World. You are either a perceiver or a judger in this dichotomy. Judgers would like to think they are the only ones that manage their time. They tend to think perceivers just mill around through the day and do whatever hits them at the time. Actually perceivers do manage their time; it is just a little loose. But, judgers should not be too confident in their own ability to organize their time, because they can become just as inefficient by spending an inordinate amount of time planning and organizing without really doing. Also, judgers can plan an item into a day that has no real importance to the grand scheme of things, but because it is planned and on their list, they will work to accomplish a worthless task. As long as they can put the checkmark on their to-do list, they will be satisfied.

Both sides of this dichotomy can be efficient or inefficient with their time. The key to unlocking the door to successful time management is to better understand your strengths and weaknesses, using that platform for venturing out into effective task completion. The following table will generally define the strengths and weakness of the perceiver and judger. This is very general, but it may help you to gain an understanding of what things you can do to work better with your spouse in accomplishing tasks for the household.

	Strengths	Weaknesses	Suggestions
SJ	• Structured and organized • Plans the work • Works the plan until completion	• Loses sight of the overall picture • Time can be wasted on insignificant tasks • Take on too many tasks • Struggles with unplanned interruptions	• Verify that the tasks fit in to the overall big picture of what you want to accomplish • Allow some flexibility in your life, your spouse and friends will appreciate it • Delegate some tasks, you aren't the only one who can do them well
SP	• Adaptable and flexible • Deals with situations that arise • Work well in situations that are not routine	• Easily distracted • May not seem to take things seriously enough • Get bored if the task takes to long to accomplish	• Minimize potential distractions as much as possible • Create plans that are flexible and have options • Let others know of you seriousness in tasks that require serious attention
NJ	• Sees the long-term ultimate goal • Can make the big plans • Usually works to complete a plan	• May miss minor details in a plan • Sometimes works too much toward the perfect plan and fails to get started on the actual work	• Realize when the plan is good enough to get started • Don't neglect spouse and friends do to overworking yourself

NP	• Sees the long-term ultimate goal • Can accomplish a lot in a short amount of time when inspired • Can be focused on the project at hand	• May spend too much time dreaming the perfect idea and fail to get started on the tasks • Underestimates the amount of time it will take to complete a task • May work night and day to finish a task neglecting all else	• Realize when the plan is good enough to get started • Break a project down into smaller tasks and set some deadlines for each task to avoid the last minute rush to accomplish a major task

Realizing how your style affects those around you can help you to develop strategies to work in a manner that is more satisfying to everyone. It doesn't mean you must completely depart from your preferred style of task completion, but it can be modified a little to accommodate your spouse. Remember, it is more effective to flex your style a little to accommodate your spouse, rather than an attempt to change them.

It can be helpful to understand how the other person prefers to work. The next sections are less on managing time in general and more on how certain types work on a task.

HOW THE JUDGER COMPLETES TASKS

The difference between how a judger and perceiver completes a task became evident to me as I taught Myers-Briggs classes for business. In explaining the differences to a class one day, I came up with an illustration that most participants felt truly reflected the differences. I will use the illustration in this book as I begin to explain how a judger completes a task.

As mentioned in chapter four, judgers typically like to work on one task at a time, working steadily on the task until it is completed. In many cases, the judger will work steadily on the task with no significant lulls or surges in performance. There is just nice steady progress being made as he works toward completion and the ever-satisfying check-mark on his to-do list. If you graphed the process, it would look something like this.

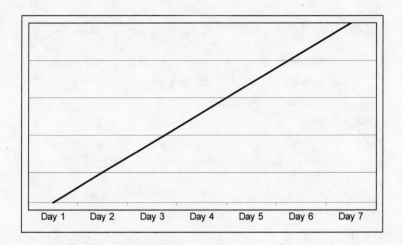

Now this is a perfect world illustration. There are outside influences that can make a judger stray just a little on the progress toward project completion. Interruptions can affect the progress. Some interruptions are favorable for the judger and some are not. For example, something extremely exciting can occur that is high on the judger's value system, causing him to delay progress. An example of this is where the judger may be working on landscaping the yard when an old friend stops by for a visit. In this case, progress will be delayed for the time being, but once the friend leaves, work will continue steadily. Still, there will be some disappointment in the judger for falling behind on the plan. Other interruptions may not be so pleasurable and will cause greater stress to the judger, who is falling behind and has no control over the outcome.

One other factor that can significantly impede progress on a task or may even delay the starting of a task is the fact that it is a job the judger hates to do. It varies from person to person, but everyone has those things that they hate to do. Judgers in this case can become procrastinators. Although procrastination is usually attributed to the perceiver, the judger will delay those jobs he hates to do. But once the job is started, the judger usually will work in the same steady manner to complete the task he may check it off his list.

HOW THE PERCEIVER COMPLETES A TASK

Perceiver task completion can be one of the sorest spots in a marriage. Judgers can become infuriated when their perceiving spouse seems to keep putting off those projects. Even more frustrating is when the perceiver has started several projects before completing any of them. Judgers should not lose hope. Perceivers can be quite productive. The challenge for the spouse of the perceiver is to learn to harness the productivity.

The key to project completion for the perceiver is based on a few things:

1. Perceivers work better when they are inspired to do the work.

2. Perceivers typically work on more than one thing at a time.

3. They usually will not work efficiently if forced to work like a judger.

Perceivers can accomplish a lot of work in a short period of time. Most of the time, no one knows when that time will occur—even the perceiver. Inspiration must occur for the perceiver to really hit his stride and get some work accomplished. But, when he gets started, there is not a more efficient person than the inspired perceiver.

Typically, perceivers become inspired when they are looking forward to doing the work or when they are nearing a deadline. As with judgers, perceivers love to get started on projects that they enjoy working on. With the rest of the projects, perceivers have a tendency to put off completion until the deadline nears. The necessity of the meeting the deadline will sometimes inspire the perceiver to complete the task in a short amount of time. If you graphed the perceiver performance it would look something like this.

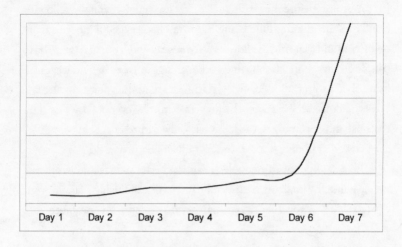

The assumption on this graph is that the deadline is on day seven. Notice that when the deadline is only a couple of days away, the perceiver kicks in and really accomplishes something. The problem that arises with this is when there are other people working on the same project and they need certain things done before they can do their part. In the case of a couple landscaping flower beds around the house, the wife wants to plant the flowers, while the husband agrees to handle the other parts of the project. Here is a sample to-do list for the project including who is responsible for the task.

1. Break up the ground using the tiller. (Husband)

2. Install plastic edging around the bed. (Husband)

3. Purchase the flowers. (Wife)

4. Plant the flowers. (Wife)

5. Put mulch around flowers. (Husband)

If, in this scenario, the wife is the perceiver and the husband is the judger, the husband may have his part of the project affected by the productivity of his wife. On Monday evening, he breaks up the ground with the tiller. On Tuesday, he installs the edging after work. They want to finish the project before they have guests over for a cookout on the following Sunday. With the deadline being Saturday, he is expecting her to work on buying and planting the flowers Wednesday and Thursday so he has a couple of days to finish. She finds other things to work on and leaves the flower bed project until Saturday. Early Saturday, she goes shopping and buys the flowers. She plants the flowers Saturday evening. By this time, the husband is fuming because he has only Saturday evening to mulch the beds. He can only hope it doesn't rain late Saturday.

There is hope for this couple. They can better manage the work and the deadlines by realizing their personality types and using a sound strategy to work well together rather than get frustrated with one another.

MESHING JUDGING AND PERCEIVING PRODUCTIVITY

Judgers tend to get nervous when they see little activity on projects that perceivers are to complete. The thought is that perceivers could do so much more if they just have a consistent plan and actually work the plan. That is the way they teach it in the time management classes, so it seems as if it should work for everyone. Well, productivity and time management is not a one size fits all. Judgers must give some leeway for perceivers and allow them to work in a manner that fits their personality. However, personality type should never be an excuse for not accomplishing a task. If the perceiving spouse promises to complete a project within a specified timeframe, personality should not be the excuse for missing it. Yet, if the deadline is met, and the project meets the promised expectations, then why does it matter the style used to get the job done?

In spite of the challenges with perceivers appearing as procrastinators, there are things a spouse can do to better manage his perceiving spouse. Most spouses of perceivers that I talk to have a desire change the way perceivers work. This is probably the wrong strategy. A better strategy is to manage the deadlines rather than the style of working. In the sample chart for the perceiver, there was an assumed deadline on day seven. To better manage task completion, the married couple should first agree on the task to be completed and its deadline. Then the project should be broken down into smaller tasks, and each one of these tasks should be given a deadline. This way, the perceiver is inspired to work on more than one occasion. Here is how the perceiver graph would look like with multiple deadlines.

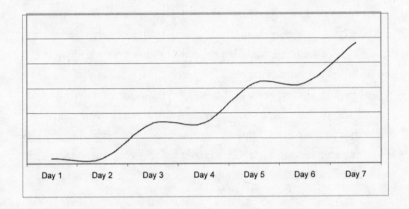

Let's use the example of the flower bed project. If we set deadlines on each part of the project, then there is a better work flow to complete the project. And, if there is a problem in the execution of the plan, then adjustments can be made before the ultimate deadline. Here is the project list with multiple deadlines:

1. Break up the ground using the tiller. (Husband)
   Deadline: Monday

2. Install plastic edging around the bed. (Husband)
   Deadline: Tuesday

3. Purchase the flowers. (Wife)
   Deadline: Tuesday

4. Plant the flowers. (Wife)
   Deadline: Thursday

5. Put mulch around flowers. (Husband)
   Deadline: Saturday

Typically, if the perceiving wife knows she has to buy the flowers by Tuesday, she will go shopping by then. However, if she does miss the deadline, there is another day that can be used to buy the flowers without putting them behind schedule.

Making shorter project deadlines can be useful, but there is no guarantee that it will work with all perceiving spouses. There is still a responsibility on each person in the marriage to honor their commitments. Remember, personality type does not dictate behavior. A consistent lack of following through on commitments is irresponsible on the part of the spouse, not a result of personality type.

All personality types have differing methods of completing tasks around the house. There are strengths and weaknesses in each type that either help or hinder tasks. Learning about your type, using your strengths, coupled with a good strategy to overcome the weaknesses will make for successful task completion with little to no frustration.

Chapter 14

THE TYPE OF DECISIONS THAT
MAKE POSITIVE IMPACT

Values are the basis for any decision that we make. Whether it is as simple as what clothing we put on in the morning or as complex as which house to buy, our values influence the choices we make. Although values are not necessarily influenced by personality type, the process we use to make decisions is influenced by type. In other words, values determine our choices; type influences how we make them.

Back in chapter 10, we touched a little on how values are the basis from which we make our decisions. Value systems and how they affect our choices are a complicated subject and not the purpose of this book. So the focus of this chapter will be more about learning the process used by a variety of personality types and about learning how to allow others the freedom to make choices in a process favorable to their own type.

THE T/F FACTOR IN DECISIONS

By now you should be quite aware that the decision-making functions of thinking and feeling are quite influential in the process of making decisions. There are distinct tendencies between the two functions.

Those with a thinking preference will tie together ideas and thoughts with logical reasoning. Linking together ideas logically can sometimes have the thinker missing the human element of a decision. This becomes evident when a husband decides it is a good idea to buy a classic car. He feels that it is a good investment because he can resell it for a profit after he makes some improvements to it. In the process, he failed to consider the effect this decision has on his wife, who he told that she would have to wait on getting new countertops in the kitchen.

Thinkers are not totally devoid of consideration of how their decisions affect others, but the thrust of their thought process is the logical connections of the ideas. That makes the human element the secondary function. This is the process my wife uses when she decides she would prefer that I avoid buying flowers on Valentines Day. You see, her logic is that flowers are even more expensive around Valentines Day, and there are much better ways to spend money. In addition, she logically sees most husbands, including those who are thoughtless, buy flowers on Valentines Day. In the cases of thoughtless husbands, the gesture is done out of obligation rather than out of romantic thoughts of a man in love. She would prefer that I show her my love in ways that are genuine, rather than in ways dictated by society.

Those with a feeling preference focus more on the values of a given situation. At times it may seem as if the feeler disregards the logical process when making decisions. That is not the always the case. The feeler usually considers the logical thought when making decisions. However, values in a given situation may win out over the logical. Such is the case when a feeling husband spends a lot of money on a surprise second honeymoon trip for his wife, even though the couple has been considering purchasing a more dependable car. He knows that buying the car would be a better choice for spending the household income, but he just wanted to show his wife how special she is to him.

The decision making process is a little more complicated than what I just presented, but it demonstrates how the process works. One additional complication is the time available to make decisions. For example, a quick decision will sometimes cause the person to rely more heavily on their preference of thinking or feeling. Whatever the decision, there is more that affects the decision than just thinking and feeling.

In a marriage, there are many challenges in making household decisions. There are the disagreements of what the decision should be when the couple is talking out the options. There is also the challenge when one person makes the decision without consulting with the spouse.

There are some decisions that should be made by one person without consulting the spouse, but these cases should either be minor or be a decision that one spouse advocates to the expertise of the other. In most cases, the decisions should be made jointly with each spouse attempting to agree with the final decision. If an agreement can't be reached, then a household tie-breaker should be imposed. In some cases, a couple could seek outside counsel. In other cases, some would feel the responsibility to make the final decision rests with the husband. Whatever the situation, the process should be determined before an actual decision is being discussed.

It is written that a person should seek wise counsel. So what is "wise" counsel? Most of us would consider that to mean a pastor or someone who is an expert in the related subject. But there is more to seeking wise counsel than looking for a knowledgeable expert. You see, some that are extremely intelligent in certain areas may struggle with applying the knowledge that they have. This would be the case of a college professor who knows the theories, but lacks the ability to apply the theory in the field. Or, it could be a case when a medical student makes good grades in the pre-med studies, but struggles when it comes to bedside manners. When looking for wise counsel, we have to consider what the Lord considers "wise."

Wisdom is the "skill" or application of knowledge and understanding. Solomon was full of wisdom, which was evident when he applied his knowledge in decision-making. God gave Solomon understanding of the heart, but with it came the wisdom to apply that understanding in judgment of his people. Read the story of Solomon and the two prostitutes in 1 Kings 3 if you would like to see wisdom or the application of knowledge and understanding. His wisdom wasn't evident in knowing there was deception, but it was evident in the effective way in which he forced the truth to come out. When the Word tells us to seek "wise" counsel, it is basically telling us to find someone who can counsel us in making the right decisions.

THE AFFECTS OF SENSING/INTUITION

Some of the poor decisions caused by misinformation can be enhanced by the function of Data-Gathering. Both the sensors and the intuitives have areas of weakness in the gathering of information that can cause poor decision-making.

Sensors, on the one hand, are generally better with details related to a subject. However, they can get caught up in so many details that they fail to consider the overall impact or the overall intention of a decision. For example, giving 20 percent of the monthly household budget for donations to an organization that helps families who have been devastated from storms sounds like a good decision. The organization was checked out with low administrative costs and a Christian philosophy. All the details fit what the husband and wife look for in a charitable organization. The only problem is that it generally didn't fit with the couple's agreement to give to a crisis pregnancy center to which they made a specific monetary commitment. As a result of letting the details blur the overall objective, the couple is not able to make their commitment to the crisis pregnancy center.

The intuitives conversely focus on the general idea or philosophy and can neglect the necessary detail to make an informed decision. Similar to our sensor example, an intuitive decides to give his monthly gifts to the crisis pregnancy center through the United Way. The sensor spouse is not happy about it, because he was supposed to write the check directly to the center. The intuitive spouse doesn't see the problem. The idea was to give a certain amount to help with crisis pregnancy, and the check was written to United Way for that purpose. The detail the intuitive missed was checking the specifics of how much of that money actually went to the charitable center. By looking at the information provided by the United Way, the intuitive would have seen that there would be administrative cost taken out of the donation prior to passing it on to the organization. The details would have shown that for writing one check directly to the crisis pregnancy center would have been a better decision.

Whether your preference is sensing or intuition, you must have consideration for the overall idea or purpose of the decision as well as enough detail to discern a wise choice. Learning your weakness and purposely addressing it *before* making decisions will move more of you decisions to wise decisions.

AFFECTS OF THE ATTITUDES

The attitudes of introversion, extraversion, judging, and perceiving, will also affect the decisions that are made in the household. Since the attitudes are typically interactive by nature, there is potential for conflict or misunderstanding when a couple with different attitudes works together to make decisions.

It's a given; extraverts typically like to talk out the decision. Since they like to think out loud, they will typically talk out the factors of a decision before and after they have a clear opinion on the matter. It may occasionally look as if they are indecisive, when they may be just the opposite. Extraverts may be quite decisive when they have enough information to make a sound decision. The discussions extraverts have are their way of working out the options and possibilities externally, while they are working on forming an opinion.

What is usually not as obvious is that introverts may also like to talk out decisions. The difference comes as to *when* the introvert prefers to discuss. Introverts prefer to discuss matters after they have been given time to process the initial information internally. Outwardly, they may look as if they are resisting input from another person. What is really occurring is the introvert building a foundation from which he will be ready to receive more information or opinions. When an introvert has not had sufficient time to process information internally, he or she will tend to revert back to the thought that has dominated his thoughts as the best choice. Here's what it looks like:

"Honey, I know we already decided on what car to buy, but I was thinking that maybe we could get a car with a flex engine," said the undecided wife. "With gas prices fluctuating so much, the ability to use ethanol would give us the option to use either gas or ethanol, whichever is cheaper at the time."

"I don't know," said the introverted husband. "I haven't heard much on these engines so I don't know how well they run. We don't even know what stations carry ethanol. I would hate to be on a trip and not be able to find a station that sells ethanol."

"That's the beauty of the flex engine," she said. "I read where you can use either gas or ethanol. We would never be stuck looking for ethanol."

"I just think we would be better off with the choice we already agreed on."

Two days later, after the husband researches the flex engine, he may come back to his wife and tell her he thinks she was right! By this time, she may have given up on the idea since she was shut down. The point is that the introvert may appear to be hesitant during the discussion of a new idea, and he or she will revert back to the best idea that has already been thoroughly processed internally—at least until the new idea has been processed.

The other attitudes of perceiving and judging will have a different affect on the decision-making process. Judgers will look at a decision with more finality than the perceiver. Judgers like to decide, have things under control, and move forward with the decision in hand. They like to put that finishing check mark on the decision and work on implementing it. Perceivers can be just as decisive as judgers at times. However, perceivers may view the decision as the best choice at this moment, but remain open for revision when new information or situations come along. This can irritate the judger who thought the decision was already made and done with. Combating this problem is best accomplished with understanding the preferences of your spouse. When your spouse is perceiving, there has to be a realization that most decisions are never completely final. Be prepared when new options come up or the situation changes. When your spouse has a judging preference, there must be a realization of the need for decisiveness and control of the situation. When the decision changes, there is a feeling of a loss of control or disorganization.

The key for making positive impact with your decisions is to know your typical style for making decisions and how it impacts others. Knowing your spouses needs in the decision-making process will help you to positively impact him or her with wise decisions.

Chapter 15

THE TYPE OF ROMANCE THAT THRILLS YOUR MATE

"Men, try this!" said the speaker in the classroom.

My blood was already at a boiling level. I had enough of hearing that all men are lousy husbands, lovers, and fathers. It seemed to me that it was becoming the Christian right of passage to be beaten down in men's sessions at church, and I knew I was about to hear another sappy tip to bring extreme pleasure to my wife.

"I guarantee that if you try this your wife will melt with excitement." The speaker in the Adult Bible Study class was building up for dramatic emphasis. "Take your wife's lipstick and write 'You're the fairest of them all!' on every mirror of the house. It may feel dumb and corny to you, but she will appreciate your love for her."

Just then, a classmate of mine leaned over to me and said, "I can't imagine what I would look like when my wife is done 'appreciating' me for writing all over her clean mirrors . . . if I was still alive!"

I laughed with him and agreed that my consequences would be similar.

But why would some men be praised for the romantic gesture while other men be condemned for the same gesture?

The obvious answer is the variation in personality type. This is why "one size fits all" tips for romancing are not always wise for men or women to follow. Had I followed the advice of a great marriage magazine, I would have missed giving my wife some of her favorite gifts.

I read *Clear and Present Danger* in the winter 2005 issue of *Marriage Partnership* magazine. I knew that I had purchased some practical gifts in the past, but I didn't realize that I had given my wife two out of the ten gifts warned against in the article. When I owned up to my shortcoming to my wife, she wanted to know my past sins that were pointed out on the list. When I showed her, she was appalled.

"I like my vacuum cleaner!" she said as I shared my most obvious blunder.

Yes, I gave my wife a vacuum cleaner for her birthday one year. I realize it sounds heartless and unromantic, but my wife has an obsession for vacuuming floors. Over the years, we had not been able to find a vacuum cleaner that could withstand the rigors of vacuuming in the Gleerup residence. However, one year I researched a certain brand of vacuum. I found it to be what my wife was looking for in a vacuum cleaner. It was light-weight, had strong suction, and was durable. It was like buying a classic car for an auto mechanic or a rare book for a teacher. I knew it was what she wanted. To this day, she loves her vacuum cleaner, and it has been the most durable cleaner we have ever purchased. It even ranks as one of the gifts she most appreciates. However, it would have never happened if I had followed the article on gifts not to buy for your wife.

ROMANCING THE TYPE

Just as it is in any other facet of our lives, romance has a relationship with our personality types. Our preferences affect what we appreciate and what we don't appreciate. Notice I didn't say that romance is dictated by our type preferences. It is only influenced by our type. Romance is not something that can be put into a formula or listed in a book of tips that will work for everyone. Romance is influenced by society and by the value system developed while we grew up. Personality type is a filter with which our experiences and values flow through to give us our desires for certain ways to romance and be romanced.

Learning how to romance your spouse begins well before the marriage. You would think that with that much of a head start, you would have it down pat early in the marriage. Yet, it doesn't work that way. Most of us must continue to learn and refine our knowledge of our spouse's needs and desires throughout our marriages. Any additional knowledge of the inner thoughts and desires of our spouse can only benefit us as we explore new ways to show our love. The benefit of understanding the personality type of your spouse is to have an insight as to his or her preferences, and how they interact with romantic preferences.

Keep in mind that personality type is only a guide to help you navigate through the possible preferences of your spouse's pleasure in romance. Just as you have had successes and failures in the past as you tried different ways to romance, you will find that you may have some successes and failures while considering personality type in the marital love life. For example, you may have a spouse who is a perceiver and loves spontaneity as a part of romance. You surprise her with a professional massage and it doesn't go over very well. From her reaction you could assume that surprises are counter to her type when in fact they are not. The problem may not be that she doesn't like to be surprised. In this case, it could be that the she does not like to reveal that much of their body to strangers. So as you navigate the dos and don'ts of romance, look deeply at the real reason for success and failures.

SPECIFICS ON TYPES

In his book, *Please Understand Me*, David Keirsey made temperaments understandable to the masses. The temperaments divide people into four basic categories using the Myers-Briggs types. They are the sensor-perceiver (SP) which he calls the artisan, the sensor-judger (SJ) which he calls guardians, the intuitive-thinker (NT), the rationalists, and the intuitive-feeler (NF), the idealists. These four temperaments can simplify some of the tendencies in people, and be quite useful in determining preferences without breaking them down into sixteen different preferences. These four categories can give us insight as to the potential romantic tendencies of our spouses.

The guardian, or those with the sensing/judging preference, is *typically* considered the traditionalists. They prefer to have their world orderly and organized. Romance for the SJ is enhanced with similar traits. SJs typically are about stability and security. Since most SJs find comfort in their routines, they find comfort in the stability of the relationship. Security can take on different looks for the SJ. Security may mean a relationship that provides financial security with a partner that follows a life plan. Security may be in the emotional side of the equation which is found in a consistent relationship. The SJ may express himself in the more traditional ways with flowers, candy, or other gifts that are viewed as normal expressions of love.

The job of the mate of an SJ is to offer stability and commitment. In a relationship with an SJ, the spouse should look for ways to show commitment to the relationship. In today's society, commitment is something to avoid. However, the SJ partner thrives on the commitment in the marriage. Tough times in the marriage are especially good for the partner of the SJ to prove their commitment and to show stability. In other words, regardless of the situation the couple finds themselves in, the SJ appreciates the same commitment and love coming from the spouse.

The artisan, or one with the sensing/perceiving preference, is considered the action oriented group. This group of individuals loves to experience the moment and enjoy life to its fullest. Romance is just one more area of life that the SP can enjoy and experience. Love is something exciting to "do" and is full of surprises—at times even to the point of being overwhelming to some types. The SP may sometimes appear to not be taking the relationship seriously, but never underestimate the playful and fun-filled actions of the SP as a flippant feeling of love. The love of an SP can be as deep and strong as other types.

The challenge to the spouse of the SP is to find a way to actively show love through the experience of romance. Traditional expressions of romance or routine romantic activity may soon bore the SP. It's not that they feel less for their spouse; they feel less for the routine activity. Finding new and exciting ways to share the romantic love will typically arouse the old romantic feelings of the SP.

The rationalist, or the one with the intuitive/thinking preference, is considered the deep thinking group that continues to seek out knowledge. This group loves the pursuit of knowledge and may come across to others as impersonal and even uncaring. Of course, this is not the case. The NT loves like any other type, but their expression can look almost mechanical. The quest for the NT is for competence in whatever they value as important. Any challenges or perceived challenge to the NT's competence will usually raise up strife in the relationship. NT's may also enjoy exploring the complexities of the relationship.

The goal for the spouse of an NT is to accept the rational view of love that he brings to the relationship. Patience is the key to romancing this group. They want to feel competent in the relationship, as with any other part of their life, so confirm their competence when possible. Tweak the interest of the NT by allowing him to explore the complexities of love relationships. The answers are difficult to come by and may provide an interesting challenge to the NT.

The idealist, or the one with the intuitive/feeling preference, is considered the natural romanticist of the four temperaments. The quest for the NF is for identity, usually focused on identity through relationships. So you can imagine that this group of individuals will focus their attention on the marriage relationship. They will forge ahead with great vigor in making the relationship all that it can be. A failure in the marriage is viewed as a personal failure, and can leave the NF riddled with guilt. Romance for the NF is filled with symbolic gestures of love, whether in gift form or in action. NF's may be challenged with the "ideal" vision of a great relationship. When the relationship does not meet the vision, they can view their spouse as not loving them or imagine there is something wrong in the marriage when there is not.

The challenge for the spouse of the NF is to help the NF gain the identity that he or she is attempting to gain. Much of the identity as husband or wife will come through symbolic gestures of love. The gestures do not have to be grandiose, but rather something that identifies or describes the depth of the love. It is equally important for the spouse of the NF to receive the symbolic gestures of love in the right manner. Disappointment occurs when the NF makes an effort to express his love, and the love of his life doesn't even recognize it. The spouse of the NF should be on the lookout for those gestures, and show gratitude for the expression.

Each of the four temperaments has distinct qualities that distinguish it from the others. Time invested into learning the romantic style of your spouse can result in dividends of peace in the household. It can also give you greater confidence in the relationship as you realize that the behaviors of your spouse may be different than that of yourself, but can be genuine just the same.

TYPES OF SEX

Sex can be a great mystery of life. It is flaunted on television in commercials, it is the focus of television sitcoms, and it is displayed on billboards we pass on the roadside. Yet, sex is not really talked about openly in a serious context. Past taboos about the subject have made it uncomfortable for some to discuss without embarrassment. Still, the mystery of flaunting it for entertainment and avoiding it in the serious context of marriage must be overcome.

Sex is also not a subject that has a lot of solid data available to the public with respect to Myers-Briggs. There are a lot of factors that contribute to our thoughts and feelings about sexuality in the marriage. Couples must come to grips with their beliefs of how sex should play out in the marriage as social norms, customs, past experiences, values, hormonal balances, and personality merge. For example, someone who has been abused as a child will have those experiences alter their image of what sex should be between the couple. As we grow up, our views can be shaped by our friends and the media. These images, whether concrete or symbolic, will help to shape our views.

In spite of the influence from other factors, personality type plays an important role in the sexual preferences of each individual. There are tendencies that can be found in each group. The table below shows a quick snapshot of potential preferences of each group. Keep in mind that these are only general tendencies. Some mates will have their own specific tendencies that stray from the general population.

SJ	SP
<ul><li>Since SJ are usually the good soldiers, sex can be a dutiful task to perform.</li><li>Can be viewed a serious endeavor.</li><li>May not be the one to initiate creativity, but still may appreciate the creativity of their spouse.</li><li>May be somewhat structured of when and where sex should occur. Although they may not be against it in other times and places, SJs may not be usual initiator of new times and places.</li></ul>	<ul><li>SPs are usually more reactive to real, concrete images of sex and love. Symbolism may not be quite as effective.</li><li>Typically view sex as a fun, action-oriented activity that is to be enjoyed to its fullest.</li><li>Usually appreciates variety in sex and can be a little creative, although not to the extent of intuitive creativity.</li></ul>
NT	**NF**
<ul><li>Since NTs like to explore the logical complexities of life, sex can be somewhat of an academic endeavor.</li><li>Typically like to search out the possibilities of sexual interaction.</li><li>May not approach sex as warm and romantic as other types.</li><li>View of sex may be complex and difficult for others to understand</li></ul>	<ul><li>Can bring a greater excitement and romance to sex than the NT counterpart.</li><li>May be more interested in symbolic images of love and sex which can peak the interest.</li><li>Appreciates the depth of the relationship that usually coincides with sex and marriage.</li></ul>

The table is for general tendencies of particular types. To find out what the preferences are with your spouse, I recommend open and honest communication, with sensitivity toward each other's feelings. Sex can be a wonderful thing, created by God for the pleasure of the couple. If you think God doesn't allow us to take pleasure in sex, read the Song of Solomon. In that book, God shows us the love relationship between a man and woman. The couple is excited by the sight of each other, they are stimulated by the touch of one another, and they are bonded by the sexual activity in their relationship.

Sex can either be an activity that bonds the couple or an activity (or lack thereof) that separates a couple. Take the wonderful path of exploration of each other's needs and desires and work to provide the other with the pleasures that only God can create.

GUIDE TO ROMANCE

Type is only a guide from which to begin your search to understand yourself and your spouse. With regards to romance, type is the place to begin for a deeper understanding of the needs and desires of the one with whom you chose to spend the rest of your life.

The illustration of the marriage of Christ and the church is a beautiful illustration of how the husband and wife should interact. As the husband, Christ willingly gave of himself for His bride, the church. We often think of Him giving His life on the cross, but it was more than just that. Here is the God of the universe, who gives up the wonderful place where He resides, to lower Himself to our status of humanity. He endured the same challenges of life that we face, so that He could re-establish a relationship with us. The New Testament is full of ways in which His bride can give of herself to show her love. She can also offer herself to the undying love of her Husband by getting to know Him better as to how He wants to be loved.

The Bible is the real guide to all relationships. Personality type is only a tool to helping us understand the needs and desires of our spouse. Learning your spouse's preferences is only the beginning. It must be followed with taking the steps to meet those needs—giving of ourselves in a show of selfless love.

Chapter 16

THE TYPE THAT LOVE CHRIST TOGETHER

In the case with this book, the last chapter is the most important in achieving the type of marriage that endures. You can have all the knowledge of personality type and apply it successfully, but your marriage will never reach its potential without Christ being an intricate part of the union. As we will explore in this chapter, Christ doesn't need to be on the side of the relationship; He needs to be at the forefront of it.

This chapter may be a little less about personality type and a little more about our relationship with Christ. Sure, the latter part of the chapter will discuss how different personalities will worship and pray in different ways, but the majority of the chapter will cover our relationship with Christ and how it mirrors our relationship with our spouse.

MARRIAGE REQUIRES SACRIFICE

My friend John Revell is writing a book about discipleship. I had the opportunity to read the initial chapter and the book outline. One of the points that John makes in his book is the sacrifice that is required to follow Jesus. Although Christians today tend to sugar-coat the requirement of sacrifice, Revell challenges us to let new converts know that there will be a sacrifice right up front.

In the Bible, Paul compared marriage to Jesus' relationship with the church. Jesus loved us enough to sacrifice His life on the cross so that we may be His bride. As the bride of Christ, we are required to sacrifice to enter into a relationship with Him. Since our marital relationships are comparable to our relationship with Christ, we need to understand that we are to make sacrifices to enter into a relationship with our spouse. We are entering a covenant with our spouse that should not end in this lifetime, but only when we pass on to be with Christ after death. This means we sacrifice having other intimate relationships with the opposite sex and sacrifice complete independence to make our own decisions, just to name two. Most of you—even those who are completely happy in their marriage—can name several sacrifices made as a result of getting married. Those of us who are in a strong and satisfying marital relationship know that the sacrifice is well worth the price paid.

This sacrifice allows us to experience the real "synergy of marriage" and a life that is full of love and support.

SYNERGY OF MARRIAGE

I love to take my family camping. We camp in a travel trailer, so many of you tent campers will claim that we really don't camp. In a sense, you are right. We basically pull our hotel room behind the truck and park it in the woods. None the less, I love building campfires and relaxing next to them. As those of you who build campfires know, you can't build a good fire with one or two pieces of wood. It takes three or more pieces of wood to really experience a good flame. The logs somehow feed off of one another to generate more flame than if the same number of logs were being used to have separate fires. The idea behind this is called *synergy*.

I've named my ministry "Sunergeo Ministries." The word Sunergeo is the Greek word from which we get the English word "synergy." The word is tossed around a lot in the corporate world, but it has a greater meaning in our relationship with Christ and with our spouse. The working definition of synergy is "people working together can accomplish more than the same number of people working independently."

The real impact is where the Greek word is used in the New Testament. Sunergeo, or working together, is found in the final verse of the book of Mark.

> And they went out and preached everywhere, while the Lord **worked with them**, and confirmed the word by the signs that followed. And they promptly reported all these instructions to Peter and his companions. And after that, Jesus Himself sent out through them from east to west the sacred and imperishable proclamation of eternal salvation. (Mark 16:20; emphasis mine)

The synergy in a marriage allows the couple to work together and accomplish much more than two single people. Together a couple can have sexual intimacy, allowing the Lord to create a beautiful child and form an even greater loving synergy. Two individuals having sex by themselves cannot create a child. Like pieces of wood, there is greater accomplishment when a married couple is joined together in unity.

THREEFOLD UNITY

> Two are better than one because they have a good return for their labor. For if either of them falls, the one will lift up his companion. But woe to the one who falls when there is not another to lift him up. Furthermore, if two lie down together they keep warm, but how can one be warm alone? And if one can overpower him who is alone, two can resist him. A cord of three strands is not quickly torn apart. (Ecc. 4:9–12)

This powerful verse illustrates the practical benefits of a marriage relationship. It describes the good return for the synergistic work of a couple. There is reference to the support system as one partner has a struggle and the other partner helps him through the situation. And finally, there is an illustration of the warmth that love brings to a marriage.

What really sums up the successful relationship is the last verse of the passage. The previous verses reference only two people, when suddenly the passage switches to the illustration of a three strand rope. Why throw a three part illustration into a two person marriage? It can only mean the presence of the almighty God. Tucked in the verse about someone fighting against the couple, God is revealed as the third person in the relationship who gives it strength. Without Him, no marriage can reach its potential. Sure, there are some unbelieving couples who appear to have wonderful marriages, but how much more could the relationship be with the addition of Jesus Christ?

When couples come to me and discuss issues that occur in their marriages, I find myself directing them toward the Word of God which is Jesus Christ. He is the One who selflessly gives of Himself to His bride, the church. He is always there to support and comfort. He shows love in ways that we can never fully describe.

A wonderful study of the relationship of husband and wife can be found in the letters from Paul to the churches in Corinth, Ephesus, and Colossae. Passages can be found in 1 Corinthians 7:1–16, Ephesians 5:19–33, and Colossians 3:16–25. In the study, you will notice the comparison of marriage with the relationship of Christ and the church. Also, in the first seven verses of chapter three of the first Epistle of Peter, you can find another passage that discusses the marriage relationship.

All these verses point to Christ as part of the enduring marriage. Some of you reading this book may not be sure of your relationship with Christ or you may know that you have no relationship with the loving Lord. I recommend making that relationship right by committing your life to Him. As it happened with your marriage, you can begin a relationship with Him by first getting to know Him, accepting His invitation to enter a relationship with Him, and committing your life to following Him by accepting His invitation. You can pray to Him right now, accepting His salvation and entering into a new life with Him. If you need help, I suggest finding a local pastor that will help you in beginning this new relationship. Adding that third strand to the bonding rope of marriage will help you in making your marriage all that it can be.

Peter and Moses both had relationships with the Father, but you couldn't consider their relationships similar. The two men of God had completely different personalities and both seemed to have the Father treat them in different ways. Notice I didn't say that God was inconsistent. He met each man's needs as an individual.

Peter was a spontaneous individual who many would say spoke before he thought. I would say that Peter thought out loud. I would consider Peter an ESTP. He appeared to be the reigning extravert of the Apostles and was spontaneous to the point of almost appearing ADHD. Several times the Bible records the Lord asking an open question to all the Apostles, and Peter always seemed to be the first to answer. It wasn't because he was the smartest, since only some of his answers were corrected. On the Mount of Transfiguration, Peter was with John and James, who were both introverted. When Jesus transfigured, John and James seemed to be internally processing the situation. Peter, on the other hand, was externally processing the event. He couldn't stop talking to the point that the Father had to interrupt him. It says the voice of God came from the cloud "while he was still speaking."

> Peter said to Jesus, "Lord, it is good for us to be here; if You wish, I will make three tabernacles here, one for You, and one for Moses, and one for Elijah." While he was still speaking, a bright cloud overshadowed them, and behold, a voice out of the cloud said, "This is My beloved Son, with whom I am well-pleased; listen to Him!" (Matthew 17:4–5)

Not only did the Father have to interrupt Peter, Jesus usually dealt with Peter in the midst of a group. This was the case when Peter denied Jesus three times in the midst of Jesus' enemies. It was also the case when Peter declared Jesus as the Christ.

Moses had a different personality from Peter. Moses appears to me to be an ISFJ. He was a structured individual, who struggled when there was a lack of structure. His introversion was evident in the time he used to rejuvenate himself. It was also evident in the struggles he had in extraverted situations. One such situation was his reaction to killing the Egyptian. His first instinct was to hide in the wilderness, rather than to lose himself in the midst of a large city outside of Egypt.

Because Moses was introverted, God worked with Moses a little differently than He did with Peter. Notice a pattern of God working with Moses in the situation of the burning bush (Exodus 3) and when Moses spent 40 days atop of the mountain (Exodus 24). God used these times when Moses would be his best—when he could internally process the situation prior to standing before a crowd. God also used Moses' preference in structure and organization. What better person for God to choose to institute the Law, but a person who thrives on structure and rules.

The difference we see in how God works with differing personalities should be a lesson for us in our relationship with God. Often, I see people try to emulate other people and their relationship to the Lord, but it doesn't seem to work the same for them. One reason may be the difference in personality.

God works with each one of us, using the personality He gave to us. As a father myself, I handle each of my children in a unique way. Although I strive for consistency with each of them, I treat each in a way that fosters growth in their own personality. My purpose is to allow them to fully develop their personality through their preferences. Though I don't fully know the mind of God, I have trouble believing that He would create differing personalities, and then ignore the differences. I feel that He appreciates the individual differences in worship, praise, and prayer that He receives from His people.

As a husband or wife, each of us needs to respect the differences in our personalities and how we relate to our Creator. One may seem to flourish in the group worship setting, while the other may get closest to God while they are alone. One may find more purpose and plan while reading the Bible, while the other may spot specific nuances that make the word come alive. One may find comfort in the worship service that has consistency and structure, while the other loves the spontaneity of an unstructured service. Whatever the preference of the individual, we need to allow our spouses (and ourselves) the opportunity to seek a closeness to God that works best for us and is consistent with His word.

The following is a listing of potential preferences based on personality type. You may find that you have grown accustomed to something outside of your preference. Remember, we can learn behaviors that are outside of our type preferences. And, I believe God places us outside of our comfort zone from time to time, so that we become more dependent on Him.

Introverts:	Extraverts:
• May prefer small group study and independent study to large congregational study • Typically like to listen quietly and give input only when it is a subject that has been thought through previously • Prayer life may be a powerful quiet time with the Lord • May prefer more meditative forms of worship	• May thrive in large group settings such as large Bible study or congregational study • May find prayer more effective if they verbalize their prayers • May enhance their Bible study when it is accompanied with group discussion • May prefer expressive forms of worship
Sensors:	Intuitives:
• May pay particular attention to the detail of a passage • May miss the overall idea of a passage when the focus is too much on the detail of the story • May miss some of the symbolism reflected in the Bible	• May get the gist of a biblical story or idea, but struggle with remembering names and locations of the story • May be more apt to find the symbolic meaning in passages
Thinkers:	Feelers:
• May lose interest when the focus of biblical discussion focuses only on relational issues • May focus prayerfully on situations and issues and forget to consider prayer for the people involved	• May lose interest in the logical biblical discussions and may get caught up in relational issues • Prayer may focus on people involved in issues and forget situational issues • Can become too involved in problems brought up in a congregation
Judgers:	Perceivers:
• May find more comfort in structured services • Prefer events to be well managed and organized • May thrive with a consistent prayer time	• May enjoy services that incorporate spontaneous forms of worship • May be more apt to find inconsistent times for prayer and meditation

This table represents natural tendencies which can be influenced by beliefs and forms of worship that were learned from childhood or over a period of time. The purpose is to learn that within a given group of believers, there are certain preferences in the relationship with God that may be exercised. Many people feel confined in their faith if every aspect is dictated by others. Free expression of real faith pleases God, and is accepted when it is genuine. He accepts the one who quietly praises his Lord with a tear in the eye and the one who freely speaks out. He accepted Peter's extraverted outburst and worked through John's introverted meditation.

When there are differences in personality type in a marriage, there are spiritual advantages. Reflecting on the passage of the three-strand cord, we can use the help of one another in an even greater way when one has strength in an area of spirituality that the other lacks. Use the strengths of your spouse to enhance the duel relationship you have with the Lord.

CONCLUSION

There is a lot to learn about ourselves and our spouses. It will fill a lifetime of learning and we still will fall short of knowing it all. But, learning about ourselves and our spouses can be a wonderful path the Lord guides us through to a fuller marriage that will be an example to the world around us.

Use this book as a resource to follow up and continue greater understanding. Remember, understanding is not useful unless it is coupled with wisdom to apply the knowledge gained. There is wisdom in developing a strategy of flexing your style to meet your spouse's preferences, rather than attempting to change the personality that God gave them.

Let us build the type of marriage that endures a lifetime of challenges and leaves a legacy of love for our children to carry on.

Contact Craig Gleerup at:

Sunergeo Minstries
PO Box 151
Goodlettsville, TN 37072

ENDNOTES

1. Briggs Myers, Isabel, et al., MBTI Manual: A Guide to the Development and Use of the Myers-Briggs Type Indicator. Third Ed. Palo Alto: Consulting Psychologists Press, 1998. Page 3.

2. Kirby, Linda K., and Katharine D. Myers. Introduction to Type Dynamics and Development. Palo Alto: Consulting Psychologists Press, 1994. Page26.

3. The Barna Group LTD. "Born Again Christians Just As Likely to Divorce As Are Non-Christians," Ventura: The Barna Group, LTD, September 8, 2004.

4. Goldsmith, Malcolm. Knowing Me, Knowing God. Nashville: Abingdon Press,1997. Page 38.

5. Murphy, Elizabeth. The Developing Child. Palo Alto: Davies-Black Publishing, 1992. Page 12.